SPACES FOR LIVING

SPACES FOR LIVING

How to create multi-functional rooms for today's homes

LIZ BAUWENS AND ALEXANDRA CAMPBELL

Photography by Simon Brown

COLLINS & BROWN

To Frederick, Rosalind, Lois, Milo and Finn

First published in Great Britain in 1999
by Collins & Brown Limited
London House
Great Eastern Wharf
Parkgate Road
London SW11 4NQ

1 3 5 7 9 8 6 4 2

British Library Cataloguing-in-Publication Data
A catalogue record for this book is available from the British Library.

ISBN 1 85585 624 7

Editor: Mary Lambert
Designer: Christine Wood
Illustrator: Kate Simunek

Reproduction by Grafiscan, Verona, Italy
Printed and bound in Hong Kong by Dai Nippon Printing Co

contents

introduction

Spaces for Living is about the way we live now. Dual-purpose rooms and open-plan layouts mean that the walls have come down between formal and informal parts of the house, between friends and family, and, as increasing numbers of people work from home for at least part of the time, between our social and professional lives. It's a more relaxed way of living but often a more pressured life – with space and time at a premium, houses must not only look good, but make optimum use of the available space and be easy to live in. We are both working mothers with busy lives: we have offices at home, enjoy entertaining and family life, and have ever-growing demands for good storage solutions. Yet we also want to live in houses that reflect our personalities.

The houses, flats and studios featured in this book are all real homes, and every photograph reflects a real answer to the dilemmas presented when decorating today. Some of the

homes have been designed by professionals, others by those who live in them, many by a combination of the two. Some are large houses, while others are exceptionally small.

Interiors today rival fashion as showcases for personal style, so these are design-led solutions to the common problems of creating a home that feels as good as it looks, yet they are equally appropriate to those on a tight budget or to more lavish projects. Tastes range from those who collect

antiques to the more vibrantly modern, yet all reflect an individual attitude to style. Some are family homes, others are lived in by one or two people, but they are all twenty-four hour living spaces, where people live, work, sleep and play, rather

than places which are merely dormitories at the end of the day. They are interiors that make it easy to talk – in this high-pressure, fast-lane world, there's often all too little time

to communicate. Yet privacy is also an issue in an over-crowded world, so space is also carved out for peace and relaxation.

This book offers answers to these contradictory, contemporary questions. Whether you are updating just one room or renovating a whole house, here are ideas and solutions that will work. Between us we have over thirty years' experience in interiors and design on magazines, and we learned a great deal while researching and writing this book. We hope you will too.

Liz Bauwens   *Alexandra Campbell*

KITCHEN

PLUS

The kitchen as the 'heart of the home' has become a cliché – but only because it is so true. People are prepared to spend significant sums to ensure that it is comfortable, practical and reflects their lifestyle. Today most kitchens do have some sort of dual-purpose function, frequently doubling up as dining rooms, play areas, or living zones.

Today's kitchen requires new thinking: does it belong in a bigger or better room in the house? Is it really practical to have the units round the sides and the table in the middle? Think in terms of 'work zones': the wet zone (washing up and dishwasher), the cooking area (hob, oven, food chopping area) and even a refreshment zone (coffee, kettle, cups). Store everything according to zone, and make sure all have easy access to water. You should also be able to move around the room easily, and everyday items should be more accessible than special occasion cutlery, china and glassware.

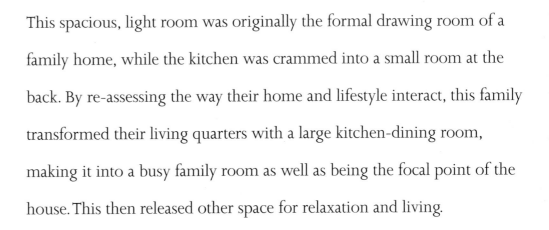

the city kitchen/ dining room

This spacious, light room was originally the formal drawing room of a family home, while the kitchen was crammed into a small room at the back. By re-assessing the way their home and lifestyle interact, this family transformed their living quarters with a large kitchen-dining room, making it into a busy family room as well as being the focal point of the house. This then released other space for relaxation and living.

This kitchen-dining room is smart enough for formal entertaining, and the well-equipped kitchen has plenty of space for food preparation, cooking and storage. The central island makes it a sociable room, where the cook is part of the conversation whether he or she is preparing a family meal or a dinner party for friends.

a fresh look

The success of this room is due to the way the family re-assessed their lifestyle after several years of living in the house. It had originally been laid out according to the traditions of 100 years ago when it was built – a twentieth-century lifestyle was now being shoe-horned into a nineteenth-century building. The main issue was the kitchen, a small room off the living room, where family and friends congregated, leaving the large, beautiful drawing room unoccupied. A separate dining room was also under-used. After a lot of thought, plus a feng shui consultation from architect and feng shui practitioner, Christian Kyriacou, they decided to use the biggest room for the kitchen-diner, turn the dining room into a smaller formal drawing room, and transform the kitchen into a television room-cum-snug. Now the kitchen-dining room is the biggest and best situated room in the house – and, as in feng shui terms it falls into the 'relationships' area of the house, it has become the perfect place for everyone to gather. The whole building flows better, because instead of cramming 80 per cent of family life into 25 per cent of the floor space, daily activities can be spread out through the whole ground floor.

the dining area

Here a Fifties' Wurlitzer adds a lively note and draws attention to the fun part of the room. There are just two or three substantial pieces of furniture: a dining table, a dresser and a fireplace. The dresser is, in fact, a set of mahogany library shelves, and, because the wood was so good, the family debated whether to paint it. It was finally resolved, and once it was painted white, everybody realized that it had been worth trusting their instincts.

The room was painted with British Standard White, a white that is slightly less crisp than Brilliant White. To add a little more definition, a very slightly darker shade was used for the woodwork of the units, the cornices and the skirting board. Such a shade variation is scarcely detectable to many, but it helps to give shape and some definition to a large expanse of one colour.

1: Storing glasses behind the glass doors shows them off to advantage, and keeps the dresser looking calm and uncluttered.

2: A 1950s' jukebox provides a colourful focus in an otherwise monochrome scheme, and it plays great records too.

right: The dining end of the room.

the kitchen

This room has two big windows, large French doors onto the garden, a fireplace and two internal doors, one leading to the snug and the other to the main hallway. This means that there is comparatively little wall space for full-length cupboards, especially as a large American fridge-freezer and a family-sized Aga take up a substantial part of the main wall. The solution, designed by architect Christopher Spink, was to have fitted kitchen units at waist height extending out into the room as a

breakfast bar-cum-room divider, providing generous work surfaces and plenty of under-counter storage. This divides the dining and eating areas quite distinctively, with the fireplace, table and dresser in one half of the room, and all the kitchen equipment situated in the other. This fitted in well with the feng shui aspect of the brief too, as they were advised to make a very clear division between the two uses of the room.

A central island creates more storage space and work surfaces, housing the dishwasher, and providing a useful place to hang

radiators. One of its pull-out drawers contains pots and pans, conveniently close to the Aga, while the drawer mechanism means that pots are easy to locate without having to search around at the backs of cupboards. Central islands, one of the most popular introductions in kitchens over the past decade, work particularly well in big rooms such as this, because they offer the cook the chance to face into the room while he or she is working, to take part in any conversation that is going on or to keep an eye on young children. In a big room they also cut down

THE CITY KITCHEN/ DINING ROOM CHECKLIST

■ A breakfast bar is good as a room divider, creating extra work surfaces and cupboard storage. It also keeps children and pets away from the cooking area. However, it reduces flexibility because it is fixed so you can't clear the room for special occasions.

■ A central island is sociable, providing extra work surface within easy reach of stove, sink and cupboards, also offering extra space beneath for storage. However, it takes up far more space than most people realize, and can be an obstacle rather than an asset.

■ Most kitchens need some fitted elements to maximize the space, but don't just accept a standard layout. Think through the preparation of a typical family meal, special occasion cooking and even a snack or cup of coffee. Work out where you'll keep things and whether things are in easy reach.

■ Deep drawers often work better than cupboards because you can pull them out and access everything easily, rather than rooting around at the back to find pots or tins.

on walking from one side to the other, and mean that you can cook with everything in easy reach. However, in smaller kitchens, they can be something of an obstacle.

The big American fridge-freezer was encased in a larger frame, with cupboard space above, and open corner shelves also provide more storage areas. To avoid a closed-off, over-fitted feel, the units stop short of the ceiling, something that works very successfully in a room with high ceilings, and impressive pediments were added on top to add a sense of proportion. The placing of the sink works well in functional terms also, its position by the window dictated by feng shui because windows and glass are both water elements and it is therefore considered wise to keep the water function close to them.

lighting

Lighting is very important in any dual-purpose room, and here the low-voltage spotlights set into the ceiling on two different circuits ensure that the dining and kitchen areas can be lit separately. Natural daylight was an issue too – although there are French windows to a terrace and large windows facing the garden, it's a north-facing room, so a skylight was added, and now sunlight floods into the room all year round. The white paint, plus the use of a relatively pale wood – maple – as a work surface, along with pale natural wooden floors all also add to the impression of good natural light.

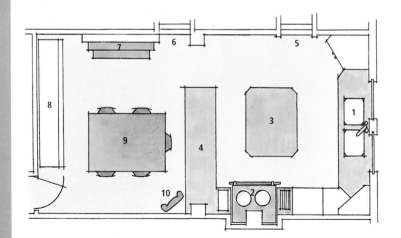

FLOORPLAN
(1) Sink facing window.
(2) Cooking range. (3) Central island, including radiators.
(4) Breakfast bar unit.
(5) Doors to garden. (6) Door to TV room. (7) Fireplace.
(8) Mahogany dresser painted white. (9) Dining table.
(10) Jukebox.

A black granite splashback gives the Aga a sleek, sophisticated look. There is also an extra ceramic hob (1) next to it to provide extra cooking facilities or to use in the height of summer when the Aga is switched off. The central island (2) has pull-out drawers containing pots and pans facing the cooker, with a central heating radiator hung on each side and a dishwasher enclosed on the fourth side. This big corner of the breakfast bar (3) is either used for eating, or as a decorative focal point with a big vase of flowers.

the kitchen/ playroom

This stylish L-shaped kitchen-playroom is also a dining room. Well designed storage means that everything can be hidden away after use, while flexible furniture, such as tables on wheels, offers a combination of options: a dining table plus work surface, an extra-long table or they can be pushed aside. All equipment, such as the toaster and the blender, is hidden behind cupboard doors which can be opened for use when in place.

These purpose-built cupboards are the key to the success of this adaptable room. At the playroom end they conceal toys, books, china and the TV.

The two matching ones situated on either side of the cooking range contain food, utensils and electrical equipment for use in the kitchen.

The working zone

This kitchen is sleek and stylish, but still a warm, friendly, family room. In many ways, it is the ultimate contemporary example of a room that doesn't feel like a kitchen. It is a design that aims to conceal, and it is the antithesis of the traditional family kitchen, with its hanging pots, dresser with plates on display and kettle permanently on the boil. The owner was determined that everything could be put away, so the kitchen was built to conceal the clutter of food preparation. When all the cupboard doors are closed, only the big range gives away clues as to the room's real function. Above all, she wanted to be able to put everything out of sight quickly and easily, so that the family never had to look at toasters, kettles or blenders while they relaxed or played at the other end of the L shape. Crucial to this was the knowledge that taking things out of cupboards, plugging them in and then putting them away again was likely to prove too much with a busy life and small children around.

Each cupboard, therefore, is virtually a mini kitchen area of its own, with special sections to house electrical equipment, where each piece can be left permanently plugged in. A pull-out shelf directly underneath extends outwards when the cupboard door is opened, offering a work surface for bowls, pots or pans. Once the

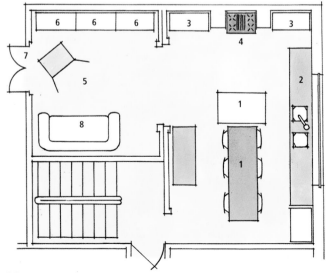

FLOORPLAN
(1) Tables on wheels that can be placed at right angles or in one line. (2) Run of kitchen units with sink. (3) Cupboards housing food and plugged-in electrical equipment, including pull-out work surfaces.
(4) Range. (5) Play area.
(6) Co-ordinating cupboards housing toys, books, TV, video and music system. (7) Doors to garden. (8) Sofa.

above: The cupboards open up to reveal a plugged-in food processor, ice-cream maker, kettle and toaster, each with its own pull-out work surface.

above: There are no obvious kitchen units above the height of the work surface. The white and steel decorative theme is easy to live with and is visually consistent; the refrigerator handles are echoed on the cupboard doors (1). The steel-edged range (2) is modern, but adds a welcoming feel to the room. Two stainless steel sinks (3) give stylish practicality for food preparation and washing up.

toast is buttered or the soup blended, it takes only seconds to take away the plate or pot, slide the work surface back into the cupboard and close the door. Very little space is wasted, because the shelves above have been carefully measured to make the most of every available space, and items can be kept close to the place where they will be used: teas, coffees and sugars near the kettle, jams close to the toaster and spices near the blender.

This policy reduces the need for a run of standard kitchen units. It really is not possible to hide the sink and drainer, so a short run of units incorporating these and housing the dishwasher, plus some extra storage, has been placed just in front of the window. Even that has been visually minimized as much as

THE KITCHEN/ PLAYROOM CHECKLIST

■ Decide what the cupboards will hold before building them. Simply installing as many standard cupboards as possible will not necessarily be the best option. Children can tidy up from an early age if it is clear where things go.

■ Build in flexibility, especially in shelving. Boxes of bulky toddler toys will be replaced by games, model-making, books and videos in only a few years.

■ Children need space to play, so keep any furniture down to a minimum.

■ Conceal all wires and keep electrical equipment out of reach of toddlers. Having equipment hidden away, as in this kitchen-playroom, is safe as well as stylish. Lighting is built-in, with low-voltage halogen spots on a dimmer switch, so there are no table lamps to be pulled over. Make sure that children are not able to pull pans off the stove.

■ Use easy-to-clean, hard-wearing materials, such as wipe-clean flooring and washable paintwork or upholstery covers.

left: The two tables on wheels at right angles to each other, make a breakfast table and a work surface, but they can easily be swung round to make one extra-long table.

1: The chairs were chosen to fit into the contemporary feel of the scheme.

possible, with a single, sleek combination tap housed discreetly over a white sink and drainer.

The two other 'kitcheny' items, are, of course, the refrigerator and the cooking range, and these too have been incorporated subtly into the visual scheme. By using a discreet steel theme (steel edging or steel panels for the cupboards), the stainless steel family fridge and the steel-edged range blend in without looking aggressively industrial or too conspicuous.

Apart from these cupboards, the major items of furniture in this room are two tables on wheels. Both are exactly the same height and width, although they are different lengths. They are usually put at right angles to each other, with one making a convenient work surface in front of the range, and the other acting as a family kitchen table. However, occasionally there is a

2 and 3: The cupboards open to reveal adjustable shelves for toys, kept at a height that means even toddlers can learn about tidying up. In future years these could hold books, games, videos or other toys. They also cleverly conceal the TV, video recorder and a music system.

right: With just one sofa along one wall there is plenty of play space to set up train sets and dolls houses. The cream linen curtains have been 'toddler-proofed' with a very broad band of darker linen at the base, so that sticky fingers can draw the curtains without leaving obvious marks.

big dinner or family Sunday lunch, and the two tables are swung round to run together down the entire length of the kitchen and playroom area. This means that as many as 16 friends and family members can be entertained together in convivial circumstances.

the playing zone

The play area part of the L shape has direct access onto the garden through French windows, which can be opened in the summer so that children can easily run in and out of the garden under the eye of an adult.

This section of the room is not very wide, and it has been deliberately kept as clear of furniture as possible in order to provide the maximum amount of space for the children to play with different toys, paint, set up a railway track or push round

a toddle truck. A sofa placed against one wall provides a comfortable seating area for some story-reading or for watching children's television.

Once again, the cupboards are the key to keeping the room calm and well-organized, even when there are small children constantly moving about. Firstly they tie in visually with the kitchen cupboards, signalling a change of priorities by reversing the steel and white theme with steel panels instead of edging. The lower cupboards contain toys that the children can easily reach themselves, while more precious china and glass is kept at the higher levels out of the reach of tiny hands. The television is also concealed in the cupboards, on a swing arm so that it pulls in and out smoothly. When not in use it is easily hidden from children and also from any visitors.

the country kitchen/ dining room

This kitchen-dining room is a newly-built extension to a two-hundred year old cottage, and is, therefore, the cottage's biggest and busiest room. The owners were meticulous about keeping the cottage's atmosphere in the new part, using old bricks in its construction and paying attention to details such as windows and doors, but they also wanted to live a contemporary twentieth-century family life in it. The brief was to make it stylish, yet in tune with a period building.

There is a casual, contemporary feel to this country kitchen because the style and colour of each run of fitted units is different. Designs are simple, with discreet touches such as the doors with carved hearts and initials. The colour is echoed in the bright, mixed china in the dining area (inset).

The brief

Although this kitchen is in a new extension the owners wanted it to be in tune with a period building and a country lifestyle, while being stylish, comfortable and contemporary. So the most important issue was that it was larger than any of the cottage's original rooms, as the owners wanted one really spacious room to open up the whole house. The dimensions of the whole extension were restricted by what planners would allow in a cottage of that size – most planning departments insist on additions that are appropriate to the total size of the property, so they decided to dedicate all the extra space to the kitchen-dining room.

Secondly, they resolved the issue of how to combine historical detail and twentieth-century life with a few clever concealing tricks. Full length doors open out to the garden in the summer, but instead of making these glass French windows, the decision was taken to make them stable doors with solid wooden halves below the glass. This maintains the size of the new windows so that they are in keeping with the period ones in the rest of the house, while opening the room up to the garden on sunny days.

FLOORPLAN
(1) Aga. (2) Built in shelves and cupboards. (3) Armoire cupboard for fridge and food. (4) Blue fitted cupboards with chest of drawers between. (5) Run of units by sink. (6) 'Inhals' dressers. (7) Work table. (8) Dining table. (9) Doors to garden.

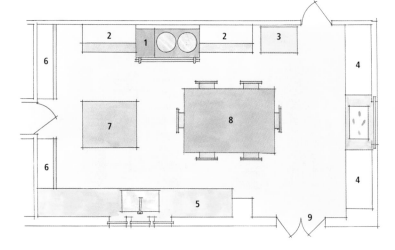

All the new windows and latches were handmade to mirror those of the cottage. When the newness has worn off, it will not be possible to tell which doors and windows were made in the twentieth century and which in the eighteenth. Dishwashers, microwaves and blenders are all hidden away in cupboards, but are easily accessible.

disguising equipment

A combination of fitted and free-standing furniture was chosen – the fitted because, with so little space elsewhere, it was essential to store everything in one room, and the free-standing to give it a more relaxed country feel. The cupboards are painted in a rainbow of different colours, yet held together by a disciplined design eye, to ensure that the room looks colourful, rather than over-matched.

The Aga strikes a homely note, surrounded by all the pots, pans and drawers that are needed for cooking. The pans hang from a rail beside this cooker, which means that they are within arm's reach – a great bonus for a busy mother. There is an unusual combination of drawers, cupboards and shelves, with drawers on a level with the Aga, and mainly shelves above. This gives the whole unit the feel of a traditional Welsh dresser, although the

1: Drawers are divided into compartments for easy access.

2: Different sized shelving makes the best use of the available space.

3: The Aga splashback is painted with hard-wearing acrylic paint, rather than being decorated with the usual tiles.

4: All cooking utensils are housed near the cooker.

5: The bold pink blind adds some zest to the softer pastel colours in the kitchen.

6: Carved inset hearts and initials are a simple decorative element on some of the kitchen cupboards.

simplicity of the woodwork and handles makes it a very contemporary solution. Surprisingly, there is no tiled splash-back to protect the paintwork around the Aga – just ordinary acrylic-based paintwork, which will quickly wipe clean, and can be re-painted quite easily if it begins to mark too much. This also adds to the impression that the Aga, drawers, shelves and cupboards are all part of one large piece of furniture. While the Aga/dresser is very geometric, an elegant citric-green armoire adds a touch of swirling fantasy, evoking the fairy tales of Middle Europe with a touch of French chateau style. Based on an original cupboard design seen in a baroque German library, and simplified to make it modern, it is a free-standing piece housing the fridge, microwave and food cupboards. Adding an unexpected touch of romance to a working kitchen/dining room is a good way to lift the atmosphere.

The sink, along with another run of units, overlooks the garden, and here the emphasis is on simple lines, with drawers of different sizes so that items can be put away and located easily. It is all too easy to have two or three drawers housing a mish-mash of kitchen paraphernalia, while seven or eight smaller drawers, each with their own few items are much quicker and easier to use. A dishwasher is concealed beside the sink, indistinguishable from the other drawers and cupboards, and the whole area is painted in soft lilac. The beech worktop is edged with stainless steel – cleverly combining traditional and modern materials.

Lastly, another 'dresser' runs along the fourth wall, and here slatted doors, each with carved hearts and the initial of a member of the family, continue the European fairy tale feel in understated contemporary lines. There is little extraneous detail, but what there is makes each piece of furniture or run of units just slightly different from the next, an essential element in the 'country' look.

The floor treatment shows the wood grain, but has been painted with a hard-wearing, light cream paint. Such painted floors can be easily cleaned in the same way as any vinyl or lino.

The colour scheme, a spectrum of lilac, turquoise and green with some vivid pink, required careful experimentation to get the right shade combination. With so much colour, details were kept plain. Doing this has kept the look clean, yet warm and family-friendly.

1: The shallow, wide drawers of the 'map' chest unit make it easy to find everything that is stored in there.

2: All the necessary kitchen equipment is neatly hidden from view in fitted or free-standing cupboards.

3: The striking 'armoire' cupboard was designed using the style of one from a baroque German library.

right: Purpose-designed storage means making special shelves for cereals and featuring narrow ones on the doors.

THE COUNTRY KITCHEN/DINING ROOM CHECKLIST

■ Pay attention to architectural details. City buildings can be similar the world over, but country homes usually have a strong sense of age and place. Brickwork, windows, tiles and fittings, for example, should be appropriate to local traditions rather than following current fashions. If previous owners have 'modernised' period or local detail, you may have to spend time researching it, but it will be worthwhile.

■ Mixing, rather than matching, is the essence of a relaxed country kitchen. Instead of following a unified style in the room, try a few different design elements or several colours. Beware of getting too complicated – simple shapes, colours and patterns are easier to place together and more in keeping with a domestic country look.

■ There's no need to keep everything hidden away, but make sure there is a place for everything – preferably easy to reach – or your room will look cluttered. Open shelves and hanging rails will always look right in a cottage setting, but too much can overwhelm.

29

colour

clock

colourful china

range cooker

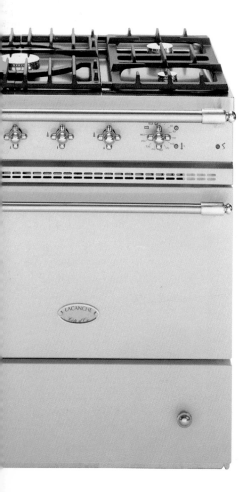

China can be neutral or brightly coloured. Matched sets are no longer essential, although an approximate theme will draw a kitchen together. Steel ranges are both traditional and in keeping with contemporary decorative schemes, part of the strong direction towards professional equipment in the kitchen.

modern refectory table

beautiful bowls

essentials

the dresser

Wooden furniture, such as dressers and tables, suggests a warm living-room feel, and even essentials, such as pans and kettles, can be chosen for their decorative aspects as well as functional purposes. A combination of high tech and traditional can look good together, especially if both are simple.

kitchen stools

striped rugs

wooden storage boxes

A kitchen-living area combines hard and soft textures: glass with wool, wood with cotton, steel and towelling. This can work in decorative counterpoint, especially if it doesn't become too complicated. Wood, glass, metal and ceramics are softened by woven fabrics, but their textures, left unadorned, also speak for themselves.

glassware

hanging storage

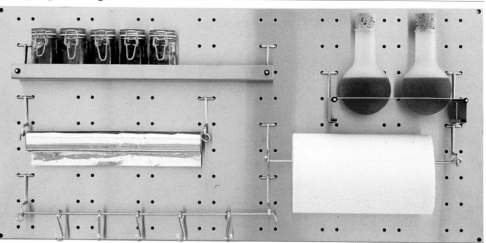

pendant lighting

curtain poles

traditional storage

Eating in the kitchen makes everyday cutlery, china and glassware essential to the look. Lighting is critical, and should be on separate circuits – good task lighting over the kitchen zone, elegant pendant lighting or candles for the table, lamps in the living area.

colourful tumbers

cutlery

OPEN-PLAN

LIVING

An open-plan home is the ultimate in multi-functional living, making the optimum use of space and light. Lack of privacy and noise are sometimes an issue, but, ironically, both very large and very small homes make work best with an open-plan or virtually open-plan layout. Apartments carved out of industrial buildings, such as warehouses, make stunning open-plan spaces, and can be difficult to divide into conventional rooms anyway. At the other end of the spectrum, a flat made of two, three or four boxy and unattractive rooms can be transformed by knocking down walls and rolling all the functions into one.

It is important to employ a qualified surveyor, builder or architect to ensure that load-bearing walls are properly supported by extra joists, and make sure that the room, especially the storage, is fully planned before starting work. Built-in furniture makes the best use of space, but mistakes are difficult to rectify afterwards.

large space/
loft living

'Loft' or warehouse apartments are the epitome of stylish living today, and this multi-purpose living space in a converted warehouse shows that such homes are not just for young single people. This spacious room can be used for relaxing, dining, working, as a children's play zone and for business presentations. The secret is to have just a few big pieces of furniture that can easily be moved, plus good storage facilities in a walk-in cupboard that is situated just off the main room.

A restrained use of colour works well in a multi-functional space – these blue sofas make a bold statement against the neutral shades. The white china and clear glass collection in the kitchen, seen from the main room, does not intrude.

the brief

This family is quite typical of this century. One, and sometimes both, partners work full-time from home. Their business activities include design work, building prototypes, administration and presentations. Children from a previous marriage also live here for part of the time. The whole family enjoys socialising, and the space, although generous, is used to full capacity. At the weekend and during the evening the room is used mainly as a play area or for entertaining, while during the day it is often wholly taken over with business activities. Switching from one activity to another takes the minimum amount of time, as toys, games and meals can be put away and audio-visual equipment, drawing boards and papers can be pulled out. The sofas can be used for informal meetings or watching television, and the long table can host either a dinner party or a meeting for a dozen people. The

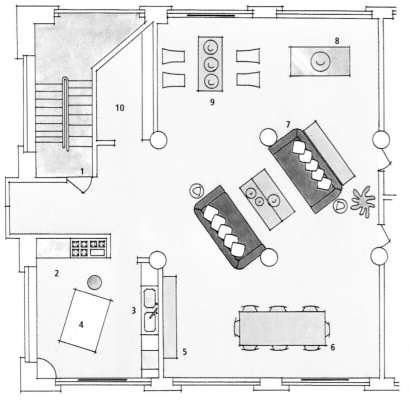

above: To keep the feeling of the room light and airy, these storage units have been suspended on the partition wall, rather than standing on the floor. The rectangular shape of the unit mirrors the lines of the partition, creating a pleasing sense of simplicity and style.

FLOORPLAN
(1) From the stairs and entrance area the kitchen is easily reached (2). There is one short working zone of sink and surfaces (3), and ultra-flexible storage/work surface is achieved with a central mobile unit (4). Dining room storage cabinets are hung on the partition half-wall (5), and the dining table is conveniently close (6). There is a central 'living' zone (7), a table for working (8) and a small conference area (9). Keeping a multi-functional space free from clutter is essential, so a large walk-in storage cupboard (10) has been built.

above: The view from the kitchen to the living area.

1: Finding the right size of furniture for an unconventional room can be difficult. Here two standard coffee tables have been placed side by side to make one larger piece.

2: Glass shelves in front of a window allow light to flood in but also give storage space.

3: The island storage unit and work surface is on wheels.

4: A steel-fronted refrigerator and steel range make a stylish, practical kitchen.

enormous amount of china, glass and other items is stored in a mixture of hanging cupboards and open shelves, with a good run of fitted cupboards in a cupboard off the main room, plus a sizeable walk-in closet.

partitions

Even open-plan spaces require some division between areas. Partitions can be fixed or flexible, and can range from whole or half walls to curtains, blinds, screens and storage units. Even furniture can act as a demarcation line, or a simple change in colour or pattern can denote a different usage of the area. Partitions should perhaps be seen as incomplete walls that do not cut out the light but which can have some furniture hung or placed against them.

When deciding how many partitions you will need, and where they should be, list your priorities. Do you need to conceal activities, such as cooking and washing-up, or to let in light? Do you need more storage in the room? Partitions are usually excellent sites for storage units. And how much space do you need on either side of the partition? In this apartment, the owners opted for a shoulder-height wall between the kitchen and living area to allow the maximum light to come in from the windows and to give the opportunity for the cook to chat to those in the living area. Yet at that height, it also offers complete concealment of cooking activities – piles of washing-up can be safely left on the kitchen side without making the main room look untidy or at all cluttered.

the kitchen

As most restaurant kitchens prove, a perfect kitchen doesn't have to be big, but you do need to look at how you live, and how you want to use it, before planning it, rather than simply installing as many units as you can fit in to the space.

The first thing to establish is the location of the kitchen area. Ideally, it should be easily reached from the outside door, so that shopping can be unloaded as quickly and easily as possible. It also needs to give good access to the dining room or eating area, as it is tedious to carry plates and dishes any distance. If you look at the floor plan on the previous page, you'll see that the location of this kitchen area fulfills these two criteria.

Secondly, try to keep the cooking and preparation area as compact as possible so that you don't constantly need to walk in between them every time you cook a meal. The fashion for having as much work surface as possible has now been replaced by identifying activities: a wet area, a chopping area and a serving area. Then work out the minimum space you will need to operate efficiently in each zone. And as food is usually prepared and chopped before it is served, you may be able to combine these two zones. This kitchen has only one run of units along the partition wall, where the chopping area and sink are located, but has additional work surface-cum-storage space on top of a movable central set of six units bolted together on wheels. This offers more room for food preparation and a big zone which can be used as a serving area. These six units are like a far bigger version of the popular butcher's block trolley, with hospital-

bed-style wheels, which lock it into position. The wheels can easily be unlocked so that the whole unit can be pushed against a side wall when necessary to free up more floor space.

It is also worth looking at how additional storage has been added in this kitchen. As the kitchen is placed on a corner it has only one wall, and that is completely occupied by the cooker and fridge. There is a small space for open corner shelves between the two windows, but in order to create more, the owners have built glass shelves over the window, and used them for storing glass. This achieves a maximum storage area without cutting out light, although having all the glassware on open shelves does mean that it needs dusting or washing rather more frequently than it would if it was in protected cupboards.

the living zone

A long table is situated at the heart of this apartment. It is adjacent to the kitchen area – the most sensible place to put it – and it is used for daily meals, working and entertaining. In a big space large pieces of furniture are the most flexible. If a desk and a smaller dining table had been placed together they would have looked more cluttered and been less adaptable.

Large-scale furniture not only looks generous, but it is comfortable to live with. Big pieces also match the scale of the room, while lots of smaller items might give the impression of a big area with very little in it. Huge sofas are indulgent when there are only one or two people are using them, but can be very sociable when more people are being entertained.

Big furniture can also be the central part of a colour scheme. In an open-plan space there are relatively few walls to paint, so the atmosphere will be created by the colour and shape of the furnishings. Here two large blue sofas act as a focal point in the room, but finding a coffee table that was large scale to look good proved to be a problem. So the solution was to buy two of them, and place them side-by-side. This is a trick that can easily be adapted with other pieces of furniture, such as chests of drawers or bookcases, if you can't find ones that are big enough to suit the overall scale of the room.

LARGE SPACE/LOFT LIVING CHECKLIST

■ Think big in furniture, fittings and finishes. Standard furniture and conventional patterns could look like doll's furniture next to high ceilings and exposed brickwork.

■ Industrial buildings are usually wide and can lose too much light with conventional rooms and corridors. Partitions – almost to the ceiling or half-height – can provide privacy while allowing light through.

■ Look for bargains. Extra space means you can use industrial or catering-sized equipment, such as sinks or ranges, which you can buy relatively inexpensively at auctions. Big second-hand furniture can also go cheaply.

■ Remember that workmen may not be used to converting industrial buildings, so if you are told you 'can't have' something check elsewhere. Suppliers may be learning as much as you are.

■ Flooring and worktops can be expensive over large areas, so check out cheaper materials, such as plywood and concrete, which can be painted, sealed or varnished.

small
space/
studio flat

Four tiny dark rooms have been transformed into a stylish, open-plan studio by architect Jason Cooper, who removed all the internal walls and raised half the floor area. A bath is sunk under a sliding bed, storage space is created on the walls, in steps and under the floor, and even an office is incorporated. This space is a comprehensive blueprint of good ideas to suit small space living.

A simple white scheme and honey-coloured wood maximize light and space in this small room. Much of the decoration is from architectural detail, such as the bookcases in the dividing wall. Leaving the splashback painted, not tiled, in the kitchen brings it visually into the living area.

a total living zone

This studio flat formerly consisted of four dark, high, narrow rooms. When architect Jason Cooper knocked down all the walls this allowed light to flood from front to back. Although still a small flat overall, he has created a totally flexible space for socialising, working, cooking, eating and bathing. Everything except the toilet is in the one room. There is an L-shaped kitchen area against the wall, a sofa and table next to it in the 'living' space, with steps up to the raised back area, with a bed, bath and an office. This bed area is not immediately visible from the living quarters because a half-height wall, with a bookcase on one side and the office desk on the other, partially screens it without obstructing the light. The *pièce-de-résistance* is the bed, which slides smoothly to one side to reveal a sunken bath underneath. The only separate room is the area in the hallway outside, under the stairs, which houses a toilet. A washing machine has also been squeezed into this space. Everything is painted white. This works well in a small, busy space as it will wear more quickly than in a bigger room, and white paint can be easily retouched.

above: The sofa with the bookcase behind. On the other side of the bookcase is the desk area, concealed by the height of the bookcase.

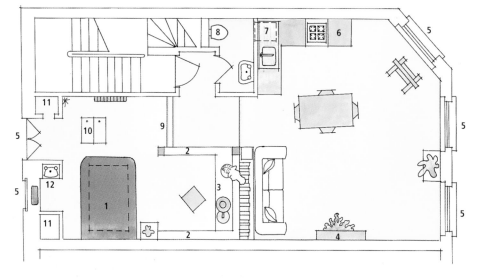

FLOORPLAN
(1) Bed with bath underneath. (2) Bookshelves. (3) Desk. (4) Fireplace. (5) Windows. (6) Kitchen units. (7) Draining board with washing machine underneath (facing toilet area). (8) Toilet in separate room, facing washing-machine door. (9) Drawers fitted into steps. (10) Hatch to underfloor storage. (11) Cupboards on either side of windows. (12) Washbasin turned sideways between windows.

1: A bookcase fitted in the dividing wall uses space well.

2: This cupboard under the stairs houses the toilet (not seen) and, facing it, a washing machine, sited in space carved from the 'L' of the kitchen.

3: Large flat drawers have been fitted into the stair treads. Here they hold artworks, but they could easily store cutlery, stationery or other items.

above and right: Horizontal 'lines' are everywhere, achieved by the raised floor, lengths of bookcases, rattan blinds, and the rectangular shape created by the dividing wall, making a narrow space seem wider. This is carried through to the kitchen, with long handles on the units, and by painting the kick-board white at the base, the lines 'float' horizontally on the wall. A removable metal strip makes a neat junction between the wall and work surface.

■ Plan before buying anything – list all the activities, such as entertaining, eating, cooking, watching television and working. Then draw a scale plan of your flat, identifying zones for each. Change it round to see if it works better.

■ List all storage requirements before you build or furnish. Don't forget clothes, books, large items, such as suitcases, cooking and eating utensils, cleaning materials, towels, office and sports equipment.

■ Measure up before buying furniture. Can you save space by building it in, for example, bench seating with storage beneath it or a platform bed with a desk below?

■ Think vertically. Cut down on furniture by using the walls for lights, shelving, peg rails, hanging cupboards and bedside 'tables' (shelves).

■ Cupboard frames and doors use up more space than open shelves. Vary heights of shelves to maximize storage.

■ Think big. One big sofa will be more comfortable and take up less space than two small pieces of furniture.

sleeping, bathing and working

Living in this studio never feels cramped because when the bath is in use it feels like being in a giant bathroom, at night it is a huge bedroom, and when the owner works at the desk, it is a spacious home office. These three functions interlock, however, because the bed slides into the office when the bath is in use.

Firstly, the bed, as well as being on runners, has drawers for storage built in its base, so that no chest of drawers is needed. Neither are bedside tables required, because small shelves with space for a book, a glass of water and a clock have been set on the wall on either side, carefully positioned so that the bed can slide

above: The bath ready for use, with the bed sliding back towards the desk area.

1: This basin, mirror and cupboard are built into the area between two windows. Placing the basin sideways, not into the room, conceals it from view.

2: Cupboards have been built around the windows, making them look deep-set. Blinds are space-saving and practical, and reinforce the 'horizontal' theme.

3: A hatch in the floor opens up to store suitcases and large objects. The space was created out of the raised floor.

4: The office area. The desk is set below the top of the dividing half-wall to conceal papers and books from the living area. It also prevents things from falling off the desk and onto the sofa on the other side.

beneath them. The reading lights are also set into the wall. All these tricks would be useful in any small bedroom – even if you don't want to go as far as fitting a bath under your bed, you can create a big storage area under the floor in the same way. There is always some space between the floor and the ceiling, but more depth has been created by building up the floor. This achieved several objectives. Firstly, it helped delineate the different living zones. Secondly, because the ceilings are quite high for such a narrow space, a higher floor improved the perspective, making the room seem wider and more horizontal. Thirdly, it gave more space under the floor for bulky storage: there are hatches set almost invisibly into the pine planking.

More storage has been built round the windows, making them look attractively deep-set. A washbasin over a small cupboard has been inset into the side of the pillar which sits between the windows, and two cupboards are on either side, one housing the boiler and the other a small wardrobe. Everything, has been built in, making full use of vertical space on walls and under the floor.

In the office area there is a desk, with a two-drawer filing cabinet beneath it, and several sets of bookshelves. As well as the bookshelves along one wall, there are also shelves set into the dividing half-walls. Not only for storage, these shelves form a useful barrier between the sleeping and living areas.

cooking, eating and living

There's no distinction between food preparation, eating and living areas because there simply isn't the space. This means that, when not in use, the kitchen needs to look as much like living room furniture as possible. The solution was a set of contemporary beech units, plus a beech worktop to echo the floorboards. The shape was laid out to reinforce the horizontal lines in the rest of the space with long, thin handles and a kickboard painted to match the walls.

The living area has been kept deliberately empty to make the room feel bigger. The table is also an extra work surface, and there is a huge sofa against the dividing half-wall, but, apart from a television table, there is virtually no other furniture.

colour

flexible furniture

curving lines

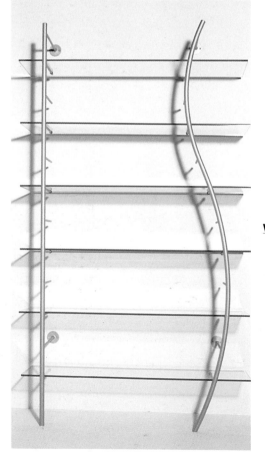

Open-plan living requires a degree of flexibility in furnishings, even in large spaces, as static room layouts are rarely possible. Tables, chests or sofas that slot together, extending or contracting according to requirements, and shelving or storage acting as room dividers all work well.

contemporary shelving

wall lights

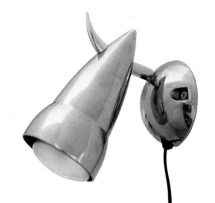

extendable tables

kit furniture

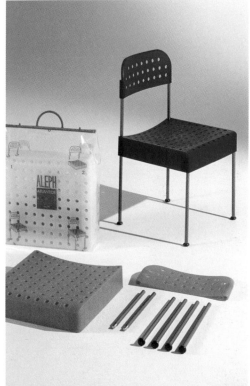

coffee table on wheels

Furniture on wheels, collapsible or kit furniture and extendable tables all offer a range of options for open-plan living. Scale is important – large rooms need bigger fittings, although smaller studios also benefit from one or more outsize pieces to prevent a doll's house effect.

radiators in all colours

modular seating

mobile furniture

Some furniture is designed with pieces that can extend indefinitely for large rooms, but sometimes the principle can be adapted for ordinary furniture. Shapes can be varied according to how the room is used, especially when items are wheeled, stackable or lightweight.

tables that slot together

vertical storage racks

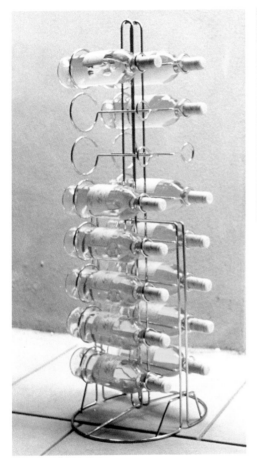

vibrant colours and patterns

classic shapes

Use vertical space in open-plan living, either to make the most of small studios or to add proportion to larger areas. Ceiling or wall racks or free-standing stacks and racks can all offer surprisingly generous storage facilities. Hooks, peg rails and shelving also make the most of wallspace.

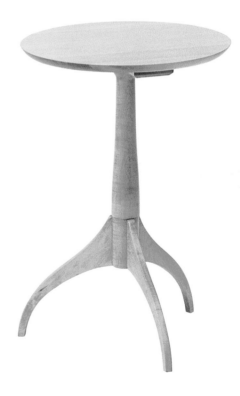

stackable seating

LIVING AND

WORKING

Working from home is a growing trend, as advances in telecommunications free people from daily commuting, but this places pressure on space. Dual-purpose rooms are the answer, with good storage so that you can switch the room from one function to another with ease.

When deciding which room to use, assess your lifestyle. Who else lives in the house? No-one can work whilst in charge of babies or toddlers, so a door that shuts is essential. Other adults may feel excluded if your office dominates the main room, or if they have to adapt their lives around your work. And do you have enough privacy? If you find open-plan offices distracting, there is no point duplicating the situation at home.

Above all, there is a major difference between being a self-employed person and running a business which involves other people from home. If colleagues and clients are frequently in the house, your family life may well be affected.

the home office/ dining room

This is a dining room that can seat eight people at a round table in the evening, and during the day it becomes a home office. The tall, narrow purpose-built cabinets in each corner open up to reveal a computer, printer, files and box storage. The 'desk' is a pull-out bureau-style flap below the computer, and the central table provides extra space at one side to place papers and documents.

Two identical cabinets were purpose-built to provide a home office and dining room storage. A central section pulls out like a bureau top, revealing a slot for a laptop or small computer. Cupboards above and below house the printer, pc systems unit, and files. The matching cabinet has space to store glasses, plates and cutlery.

55

■ Dining chairs should only be used for brief periods. Otherwise use a stable office chair that is height and back adjustable, with castors and a swivel action. Arm rests should also be adjustable.

■ You should work facing your computer, never twisted to the side. Feet should be flat on the floor or on a footrest, with your eyebrows in line with the top of the screen.

■ Do you have enough power points? When concealing equipment, drill holes for cables at the back of shelves or cupboards, and ensure airholes if cupboard doors are left closed – electrical equipment gets hot! Do not convert antique furniture – the work would affect its value.

■ To calculate storage, list the items you use daily over a week, for example: magazines, pens, stationery and books. If you use it often, it should be easy to reach. Boxes, baskets and drawer dividers ensure that space is used effectively.

■ A hands-free option prevents neck-strain if you use the phone regularly.

the brief

This room has three functions – it is the main entrance hall of the house, it acts as a formal dining room for dinner parties, and it is a home office for a busy stylist and working mother. Post is left on the table in the morning, then the right-hand cabinet is opened up to reveal a computer, filing system and printer, so that any correspondence can be answered, sorted and filed. Letters and documents are written on the computer, and swatches and invoices are stored on the shelves. This home office is essentially an administrative centre, used only for a few hours a day, so it needs less storage than a full-time business would. When work finishes, only a few moments are needed to pack papers away in their files, fold up the bureau flap and close the cupboard doors before laying the table for a dinner party. This doesn't happen every day, as most family meals are eaten upstairs in the kitchen-dining room, but the office element is compact enough, and also sufficiently well organized, to switch from one function to the other with the minimum of fuss.

the furniture

For most people, concealing the computer and its associated equipment is the key to a successful dual-purpose room. There is an increasing number of home office cupboards on the market, but in this dining room/office, the owners had furniture specially commissioned. Here two tall, narrow cabinets, one with a pull-out desk and computer inside, and the other with mixed office and dining room storage, have been commissioned to stand in each corner of a small square dining room. A circular table makes the most of the central space for dining, and seats eight people. During the day the same table can be used for meetings or as extra work space when there is a lot of paperwork.

Commissioning furniture need not be costly, and often offers good value for money. The cupboards here are made of inexpensive mdf (medium density fibreboard), and having them made ensured that they fit exactly into the space. The stylish

1: A mobile filing cabinet can be wheeled out of sight.

2: Document boxes use vertical space well and contain miscellaneous paperwork.

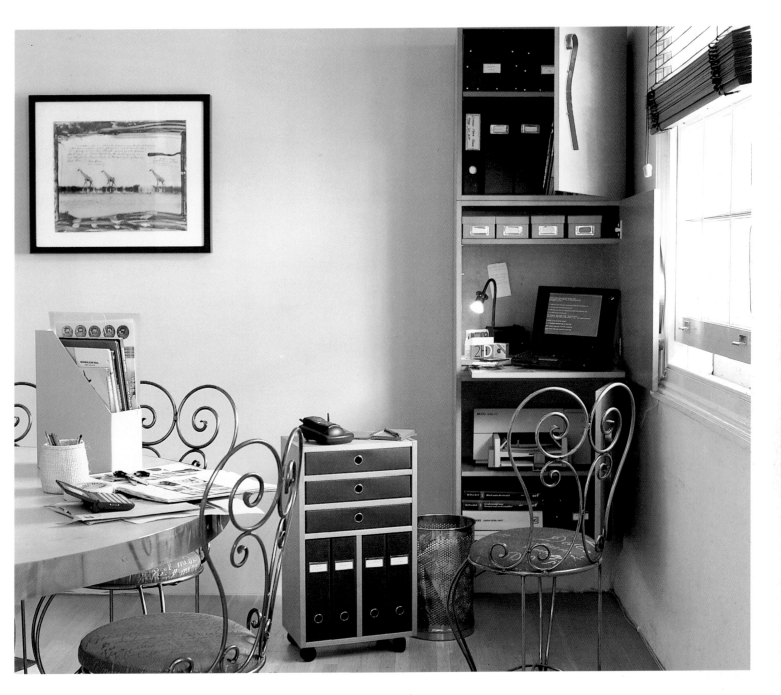

above: The dining table functions as an extra work area and it can also hold client meetings and host dinner parties. The soft lilac walls work for day or evening.

The blinds at the windows lend a clean, professional look. They are also effective at filtering sunlight from the computer screen, and save more space than curtains.

handles help dispel any 'office' feel, and the tall, thin shape utilizes vertical space, freeing up floor area for the large round table. Had the owners adopted the more conventional layout of a desk-high run of units along the wall, there would have been less room to place the table and chairs, and the 'office' look would have been much more noticeable.

Furniture-makers or carpenters can be found at all price levels, although it will always be more expensive than buying from the very cheapest mass-market shops. Ask around locally for recommendations – word of mouth is usually an effective way of ensuring good workmanship, and in Britain The Crafts Council (see page 149) also holds a listing of craftspeople. When commissioning a carpenter or furniture maker, ask to see pieces of previous work or to look at a portfolio of past work. When discussing what you want, be as precise as you can, and write the brief down. It should include all the functions you will need from the piece of furniture and the equipment you want to house. If you have any photographs from magazines showing the style you like, attach them. If someone is producing original designs, indicate what your own tastes are, for example, contemporary, traditional, Shaker or classic. Always ask to see preliminary sketches, and check such measurements as the computer, keyboard, range of opening door, room for yourself. Never assume that the craftsman knows what is in your mind, and make sure you understand exactly what is planned, and the price that is agreed, before giving the final go-ahead. When the piece is delivered, check the stability and strength, especially hinges and joints, before making the final payment. Finally, do understand that commissioning work is not an instant process – a desk may be delivered from a shop in ten days, but it may take weeks or months to complete a piece of furniture from scratch. However, the result will usually be ten times more satisfying, and in the case of difficult dual-purpose situations, it may be your only option.

lighting

The type of lighting needed is critical in both an office and a dining room, and they have directly opposing requirements. An office needs good overall light plus task lighting, such as an adjustable desk lamp (not an ordinary table lamp, which gives a glow rather than a practical directional beam). Computer screens should be shielded from glare. A dining room, in contrast, works best with low, intimate light and candles. This dining-room-office has low-voltage halogen spotlights in the ceiling, which are operated on a dimmer switch to offer bright, daylight-quality light during work hours, or a warm soft glow in the evening. A desk lamp supplies the directional light. You also have to control the sunlight – it shouldn't reflect into your eyes or onto the computer screen. Blinds, as used here, are usually more effective than curtains, and they keep the atmosphere business-like during the day. Blinds are also space-saving in a small room, such as this one, so they work well all round.

colour

A dual-purpose office-dining room presents a different challenge to a single use dining room or office. In a dining-room that is mainly used at night, strong or vibrant colours are often used to add warmth, but if the room is also used during the day, this may not be appropriate. Before choosing a vivid shade or a busy wallpaper do think about whether you can work and live with it all day every day. That doesn't mean you have to choose a bland colour, the right shade will help to dispel any office grey. An office-dining room has great potential for clutter, so simplicity (using just one or two themes or colours) is usually the best policy. Here, one wall has been painted a soft lilac while the other walls are white, and the rest of the furniture is limited to natural wood or metal shades, which links the wood of a dining room with the more high-tech metallics of an office.

To distract the eye even further from any office clutter, a few splashes of vibrant colour – the vivid pinks and purples of the chair seats, and a big bunch of flowers – have also been added to the room. When the owners get bored with the scheme and want to ring the changes, they can just re-paint one wall and change the dining chair seat covers, to end up with the ultimate solution for flexible living.

storage

Most offices need a combination of boxes, files and easily accessible trays and pots. All can now be bought in a wide range of colours, or you can stick to classic neutrals, such as black, beige, grey or white. They can either be concealed behind cupboard doors, placed on wheels to be wheeled aside, or furniture – from entire cupboards to simple blanket boxes – can be bought or adapted to hold them. A good rule of thumb is to work out what you need, but be generous and make sure there is scope for expansion as time goes on.

FLOORPLAN
(1) Table. (2) Purpose-built dining and office storage cupboard. (3) Storage cupboard with pull-out desk. (4) Mobile filing cabinet.

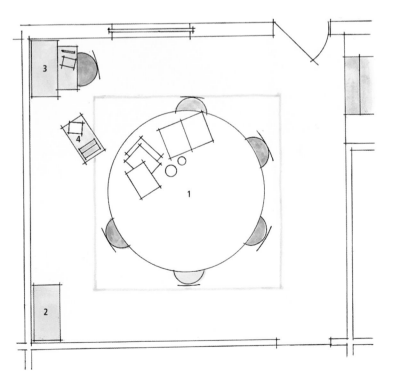

above: Flowers and candles complete the finishing touches of the conversion from office to dining room, and visitors are unlikely to realize that this room is used as an office during the day.

the office/
living room

This large, stunning room is central to both a home and a flourishing business. Designed by architect Gunnar Orefelt, it is more than just a home office, it is a client meeting room, a living room for relaxing, and a dining room for family eating and occasional large parties. To one side is the kitchen and family area and to the other, the main office of a busy architectural practice.

White walls are light and professional, but a living room needs colour. Here panels of vivid terracotta and blue offer a focal point for the eye and a background for pictures, while the surrounding areas stay neutral. The computer is not concealed, but overshadowed by a contemporary painting.

THE OFFICE/LIVING ROOM CHECKLIST

■ Look ahead five or ten years. Cash flow and flexibility mean you can't always move immediately if the business grows. Build in scope for expansion. And your family situation may change – you may marry or have more children. Plan how to adapt.

■ A separate entrance for colleagues and clients is an important consideration. The office also needs its own basic kitchenette and toilet to preserve family privacy.

■ Ensure that the office and home can work independently of each other. A separate building, such as a converted barn, is ideal, but, if not, clear division between home and office means that you can switch off more easily.

■ Divide storage into short and long term. Think ahead, six years' worth of accounts may need to be stored in a secure outhouse or a shed, for example. Even short-term storage expands quickly. Double your initial calculations.

■ Plan how you will cope with a rush job, late working or more staff, without taking over the house completely.

a home to a business

This is the headquarters of a busy architect's practice as well as a home, in contrast to the previous office-dining room, which was on a much smaller scale and was a home office for one self-employed person. It is essential to recognize the difference when you are planning to work from home because the demands on space and equipment are completely different, and the need to keep a defining line between your personal life and your work becomes far greater. Don't under-estimate how resentful even the most supportive members of your family can become if they feel that their home has been completely invaded by your work, particularly if you have colleagues visiting, employees working there or long client meetings. It is less difficult if you live with someone who goes out to work themselves, although a sudden rush or a project that requires all-night working can invade their precious private time as well as yours. Anyone who is based

above: It's hard to tell where family books and videos stop and architectural files begin. Suspending the shelves centrally on the wall helps prevent them looking too dominating, and the radiator underneath echoes the shape.

at home, such as a mother with young toddlers, or someone working at home in a different profession, may well feel that her home is no longer her own. Either way, it is important to build in as much division between home and the business as possible, and you too will feel the benefit when you want to switch off.

This large room is literally the link between the architect's offices to one side, and the kitchen and bedrooms on the other. Originally it was designed to function as a meeting room and research library for the offices, while being combined with a dining room and living room for the family. As a generous room with a folding table there was scope for large parties – either professional ones given by the practice or just social occasions. However, as the business expanded, it became necessary to move a desk and workstation into one end of it, and to use some of the family storage for files and papers. Fortunately, the flexible design and the simple fittings mean that this still looks streamlined and stylish, and the two fuse seamlessly into one.

above: The coloured panels behind each picture were painted in an afternoon, and could be changed again equally quickly.

1: A few striking pieces of art, such as this painting by Sally Greaves-Lord, are on a large scale to match the room.

2 and 3: The white table folds in triangles, so that it can be used for big client meetings or for dinner parties.

4: Many books are stored on the shelves. The rolled drawings are due for long-term storage.

furniture and fittings

A business run from home, as opposed to a home office, has to be much more hard-wearing than a home, and this has an impact on everything you buy, from flooring and paintwork to chairs and tables. This is mainly because a business generates more people. For example, a meeting with more than six colleagues could happen twice a week, whereas few homeowners would have a dinner party for that number so often. People also treat a business area differently, not out of bad manners but because they're concentrating on work, rather than their environment. So they are likely to do things such as leaning back on the chairs to make a point at a meeting, walk in with dirt on their shoes, and so on. It may not sound as if it makes that much difference, but architect Gunnar Orefelt estimates that the wear and tear on company furniture and fittings is about four times as much as that on home furnishings. This doesn't mean you have to buy office furniture,

FLOOR PLAN
(1) Desk and pc. (2) Extendable dining and meeting table. (3) Long shelving for books and documents. (4) Living zone. (5) Decorative panels of vivid colour.

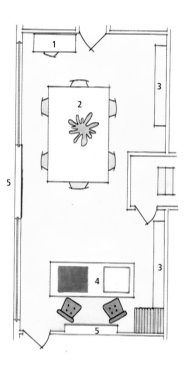

right: Look at contemporary styles to find well-designed, hard-wearing contract furniture, but that doesn't mean that your home has to be entirely modern in feel. Here chairs by Scandinavian designer, Bruno Mathsson, sit happily side-by-side with a traditional oil portrait.
far right: Splashes of colour, such as a vase of bright flowers, distract the eye from office equipment.

but it is worth checking out contract suppliers or companies that supply both homes and offices, and discussing how well the furniture is built to wear before buying it. Today's movement towards contemporary furniture is an enormous help, because you are more likely to find well designed contract furniture that will also look good in a home environment. Think about how the furniture will look at the meeting as well as in the dining room; for example, some kitchen chairs may not look professional enough for a meeting. On the other hand, elegant fabric-covered dining room chairs may not last well. The table, too, should be a flexible size and hard-wearing so that you don't worry about any surface stains when you are working.

Flooring is another key issue. Here the floor is a hard-wearing beech, but there are many cheaper versions on the market, some of which will not stand up to extensive wear. Wooden floors will need re-sanding and varnishing every few years, so if you buy a veneered wooden floor, check the depth of veneer and how often you will be able to restore it. There is a huge supply of contract flooring, ranging from the sisal and seagrass floorings to plain and patterned carpeting intended for hotels, linoleum (which can be laid in any pattern you like), and other tiled, wood or vinyl flooring. You should be able to achieve almost any effect you like, but do check that it is suitable for heavy use.

You will probably even need to re-paint more often, especially if you want to give a smart impression to clients. This makes wallpaper a less suitable option, and may limit your colour scheme to something simple and easily matched, such as white, which can be used to touch up one wall or a heavy-duty area without worrying about matching up tones. You can liven the look by painting one wall or a panel in a different colour. Here these panels of vivid colour are used to add vibrancy to an all-white scheme, but they could be painted over in an afternoon.

left: A raised floor level denotes a casual seating area, and the 'living-room' end of the spacious room.

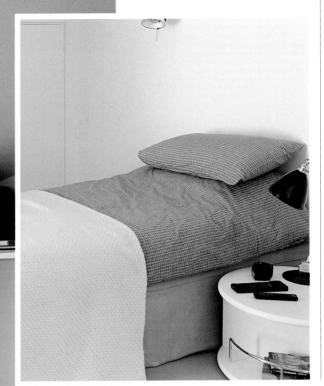

the bedroom/ study

This bedroom-study was carved out of the roof to give a teenage boy his own room. Although the house's floor area was generous, the roof slopes steeply, so the architect, Barbara Weiss, had a very restricted space to convert. The most important element in the study is the built-in storage, which runs virtually all round the room. It is so extensive that there is no need for any furniture other than a bed and built-in desk area. Leftover cupboard space is used by the family for long-term storage.

Everything in this bedroom-study is built in: there is a niche for the TV and video cabinets, with pull-out drawers beneath for videos.

Different sized cupboards in the room store clothes and larger items such as suitcases. The bed (inset) can easily be moved around the room.

room for growth

Sleeping and working in the same room is not ideal, but it is often the only option for students who have exams looming. Here the extensive and carefully planned storage means that everything can be tidied away easily, to keep the two worlds separate. Nothing is more distracting than being unable to find your notes because they're lost among your clothes. The rooms of children and teenagers are often the smallest or most awkwardly shaped in a house, and this is when it is usually more efficient to build all storage in, rather than place bookcases and chests of drawers against a sloping wall.

This kind of storage needs to be thought out before the first shelf is cut. Each shelf and drawer will have to be purpose-made to fit its slot, as the variable shapes and sizes mean you don't have the option of adjustable shelving. Drawers can be varied in size: drawers divided into sections will keep CDs and videos tidy and easy to see, while bigger drawers can take bulkier stuff. Don't be tempted to make the drawers and shelves without measuring out what has to go inside – you'll just waste space and even find yourself with drawers that can't be used for much. Shallow drawers can take pens and pencils, make-up and miscellaneous small items, medium-sized drawers are suitable for clothes,

videos, CDs and books, while larger ones can take sweaters, bedding, and so on. Small, but deep cupboards can take suitcases, while full-length hanging space is likely to be scarce in such a room – work out where it can fit first and build the rest of the storage around it. TVs, videos and other electronic equipment can be built into open shelves – just plan the wiring so that it is out of sight. A sizeable desk can be built cheaply by cutting a large piece of wood to rest on two filing cabinets or chests of drawers.

These cupboards almost disappear and become part of the wall because all the decorative detail on them has been kept to a minimum, and they have been painted the same brilliant white as the rest of the room to minimize the room's smallness.

total storage solutions

Many people look at their roof to see if they can expand upwards – especially as older children need somewhere where they can entertain and work, rather than just sleep and play. Often this is an excellent solution. However, it is not necessarily simple. In many places, there are planning restrictions on what can be done in traditional houses, and the importance of maintaining 'the roofline' is something that is growing increasingly crucial in

1: A roller blind protects the dormer window from glare.

2: Wall lighting saves space and means no side tables are needed.

3: A structured office chair proves you can be ergonomic and stylish.

opposite: The built-in desk has been planned to maximise the width of the window area.

THE BEDROOM/STUDY CHECKLIST

■ Planning permission is your first problem, as many planners want to protect the 'roofline' of their towns. Even if roof conversions exist in your road, a similar style may not be allowed as all regulations are being tightened.

■ Employ an architect to make maximum use of a difficult space. You may be granted planning permission provided that you don't overlook neighbours, so the placing of the windows can be critical.

■ Even if the attic covers the entire floor area of the house, a pitched roof will mean that only a percentage of the space is made available.

■ Insulation and ventilation are critical, so don't try to skimp on them.

■ The size and tread height of the stairs will be governed by regulations, so stairways may take up much more space than you had planned. You will not be allowed pull-down ladders.

■ With a pitched roof it is normally more effective to build in storage, rather than trying to fit freestanding units.

many world cities. However, today, most architects accept that a roof extension can be built within the framework of the building, with small dormer windows or skylights that are scarcely noticeable. In any area where planning permission is needed, you need to ensure that any exterior alterations will fit in with your building's style. It is worth noting that you are unlikely to get planning permission for a roof extension just because a neighbour has one. These controls are tightening everywhere.

Then consider restrictions inside. Firstly, with sloping roofs, you can only stand in a small area. Most countries have legislation on the room's height, and a roof extension will have to meet these.

Secondly, you will have to give up space on the landing below, or possibly even give up a small room to make a staircase. Where and how you erect the stairs will also be subject to planning controls that will restrict the size of tread, the stairs' angle and the head height in any one place. Staircases must be permanent – a loft room is not allowed with a pull-down ladder.

Thirdly, you will have to improve the heating and ventilation, as most roof areas are cold in winter and hot in summer. This should help the house below, as less heat will escape through the roof with better insulation. Even if your window size is restricted by planning controls, it may be possible to replace a roof section with double-glazed conservatory glass that will make good use of overhead light. Skylights can also be better for light than a dormer window.

1: A shelf neatly tucks under the eaves to hold all the teenager's CDs.

2: A table on wheels can be moved easily around the room, if necessary.

right: The movable bed is the only major piece of furniture that is situated in the room.

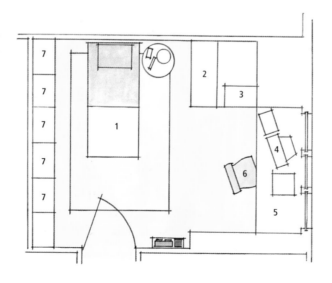

FLOORPLAN
(1) Bed. (2) Built-in cupboard for TV and video. (3) Cupboard under eaves. (4) Computer. (5) Desk. (6) Chair. (7) Fitted cupboards under eaves.

3: Carefully planned, built-in shelving has created a neat niche to store the TV and video recorder.

4: Plenty of light floods into the bedroom/study from a glass roof that is over the hallway.

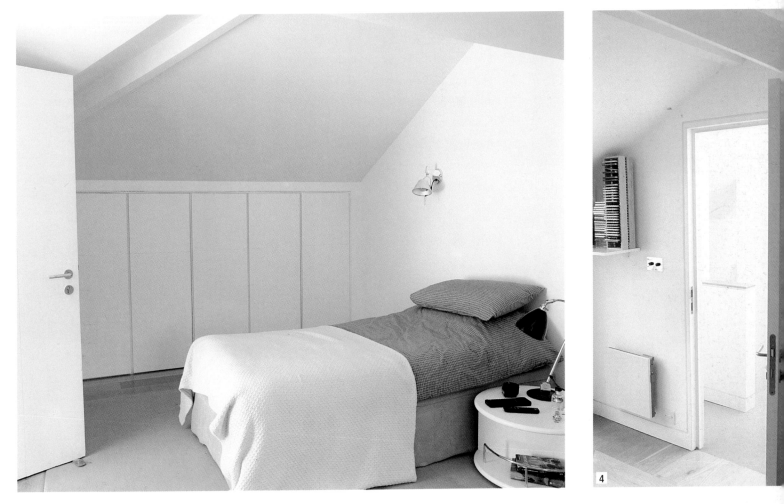

colour

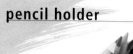

pencil holder

sisal storage baskets

dynamic shapes in cabinets

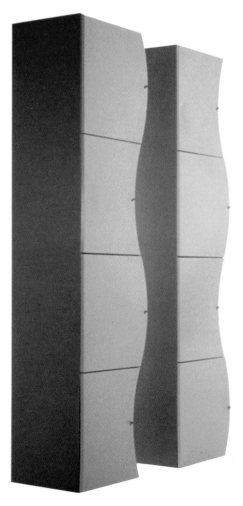

decorative touches

Create your own ideal storage system by collecting and adapting these basics. Boxes and baskets provide essential storage, and cabinets or filing units can double up as storage and room dividers. Measure up books, files and boxes when building shelves for customised storage solutions, and stack the most frequently used items closest to hand.

flexible furniture

horizontal drawer handles

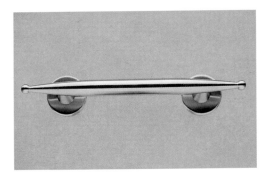

storage drawers

pocket calculators

curved filing cabinets

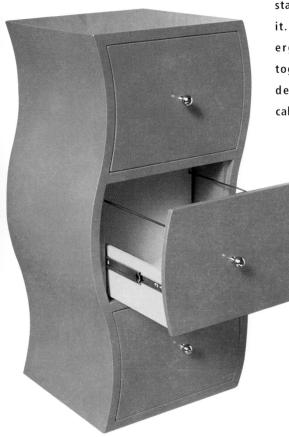

compact seating

The design of furniture for the workspace should be of as high a standard as the furniture that surrounds it. Colour, shape, style, function and ergonomic considerations all work together for a true home office. Add detail, such as different door and cabinet handles, for individuality.

flexible desk lighting

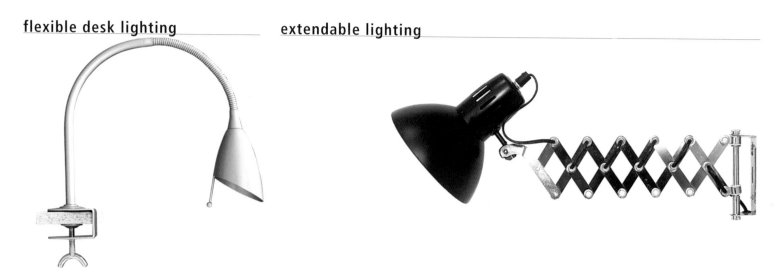

extendable lighting

curved shelving

Task lighting is essential in any work zone. Fix to the desk or wall to free up space and ensure direct light where it's needed most. Noticeboards and pin-boards offer instant aide-memoires and a quick way of storing lists, notes or useful addresses. Tables and desks should be expansive and comfortable.

noticeboards

table-cum-desk with drawers

ergonomic seating

filing cabinets on wheels

adjustable work tables

antique filing cabinets

There are beautiful old wooden desks, cabinets and chairs, sourced from pre-War offices, to be found in antique and junk shops, but always check they are sound, ergonomic and comfortable. Adjustable furniture and furniture on wheels are both useful in dual-purpose rooms. Divan beds offer a clean-lined alternative to bulky sofa beds.

divan bed/sofa

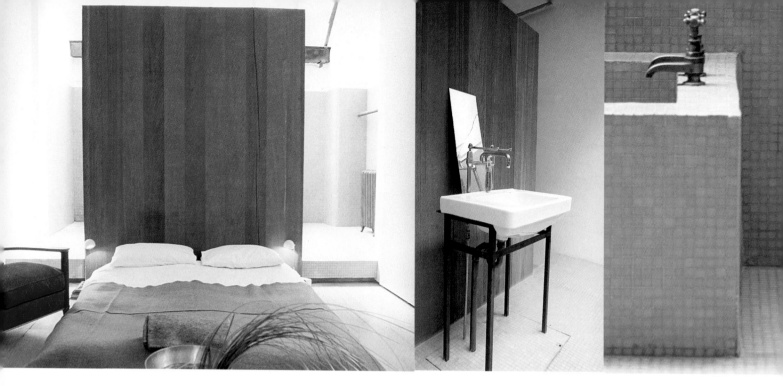

BEDROOM

PLUS

The bedroom is the real comfort zone. We spend up to one-third of our lives there, yet it is a room with contradictory requirements: relaxing yet organized, informal but well-planned, stylish and comfortable. It's an intensely personal place, but it does waste space to leave it unused for two-thirds of the day.

Dual-purpose solutions include bedroom-bathrooms, bedroom-playrooms and bedroom-studies. For many people, an en-suite bathroom is now a must-have, but rather than carving a small, dark box out of a corner, optimize space by having a bath and basin in the bedroom. It retains a room's original proportions and makes it easier to move around, although it is a solution for a master bedroom, not a family bathroom.

The bedroom-study can give teenagers the privilege of having their own space and privacy, and spare rooms can also be used as office spaces, although your own main bedroom will not be a restful choice as an office.

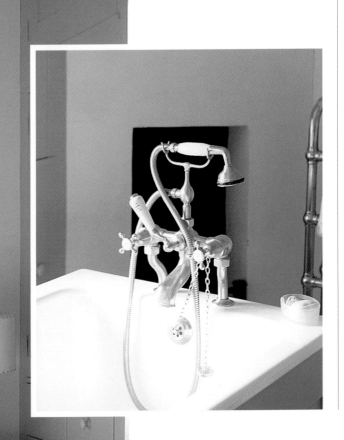

bed/bath: all in one

Here bed and bath are situated in one generous, flowing space, without any division between the two functions. Built-in storage on two walls enhances, rather than detracts from, the room's original proportions. On one side, cupboards have been taken from the adjacent spare bedroom, with doors cut into the wall to open into this room. On the other, cupboards and drawers surround the windows. Clutter can be cleared, leaving the bed and bath as focal points.

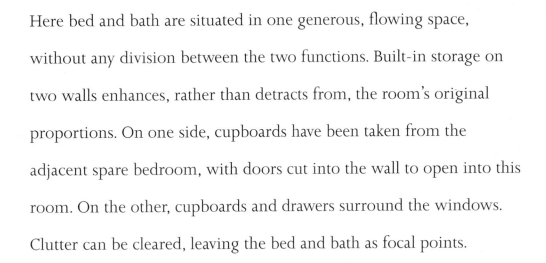

Combining a master bedroom and bathroom can be the perfect solution to making the best use of space for storage in a limited area. A cradle shower attached to the bath is in a matching Victorian style. This is the best option to link the bath visually with the metal bed-frame.

the brief

This is the master bedroom of a period family home, which had been changed into two rooms – a bedroom and a bathroom – in earlier years. Although the rooms were a reasonable size, they were not large, and once furniture, such as chests of drawers, wardrobes, side tables and fitted cupboards, was added, space had become quite limited. The owners had enjoyed an open-plan bath in their bedroom in an earlier house, and decided to knock down the wall between the two rooms.

Once they had done so, the line of the floorboards showed that they were, in fact, restoring a big, light room to its original proportions, as well as maximizing the existing floor area. Now, instead of facing a tiled wall and listening to the roar of the extractor fan when they have a bath, they can lie in the hot water and relax by watching the changing seasons in the garden through the bedroom windows.

The basic principle of having bathing facilities in your bedroom is centuries old. Houses were not built with purpose-designed bathrooms until the nineteenth century, and a wash-stand, or table with a bowl of hot water, was an established sight in bedrooms. Baths were often portable, and placed in front of a fire. Even after bathrooms became standard, the idea of having a washbasin in the bedroom was customary, but now that even quite modest homes are expected to have two, possibly three, bathrooms this is dying out. So you could view the bedroom-bathroom as the re-introduction of an old custom. There is one aspect, however, which even the least inhibited prefer to keep private – the toilet. Here it is located in a small walled-off corner of the room, with its own door, near the bath and washbasin. Some people may prefer to conceal it behind a half-wall, but if this is the case take noise into account as well as the sight line.

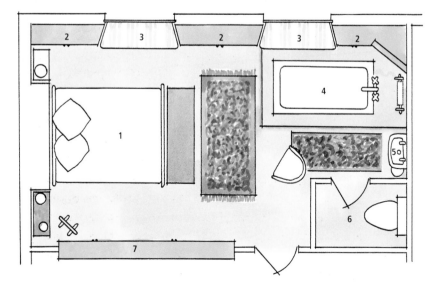

FLOORPLAN
(1) Bed. (2) Built-in cupboards
surrounding windows.
(3) Window seats with radiators
underneath. (4) Bath. (5) Washbasin.
(6) WC. (7) Cupboards using space
borrowed from the adjacent room.

1: A separate toilet is normally essential for privacy .

2: The chest at the foot of the bed provides seating and additional storage.

3: This wall of cupboards was built in the adjacent room, and these are doors which have been cut into the wall.

4: The washbasin in the corner is a similar Victorian design to the bed-frame and the bath. The wall-lights above are sealed in and cannot be reached from the bath.

above: A gentle angle at the window edge of the cupboards allows more light in. Hanging space and drawers break up the cupboards and suggest panelling. Note how the taps and the bed-frame link the bath and bed together in a Victorian theme.

the furniture

This room has stylistic unity, which is a key point to remember when combining two functions in one space. The wrought iron bedstead and Victorian bath and taps are essentially both white, and have the same feel to them as they come from a similar era. A modern bath with a Victorian bed, or vice versa, would have been less successful. This doesn't mean that the style has to be Victorian, but it is a reminder that once you have established a style, then it is usually better to stick to it. The extensive built-in cupboards and drawers ensure that the room stays tidy, and free of clutter, as the owners made a deliberate decision to create a room that needed very few pieces of furniture in order to maintain the feeling of space. There are only two bedside tables and a chest at the end of the bed – even chairs are not needed because of the window seats. This makes the windows, and the view outside, a major decorative feature in the room, drawing the green of the trees inside to blend with the three shades of green in the room.

the practicalities

Water needs a slope to drain away, and one reason why baths are often flush against the wall is that they are closer to the waste pipe in this position. However, you can place a bath in any position in a room. If there is enough space between the floorboards and the ceiling below, the pipes can run below the floor at the correct slant, or, if not, the bath will have to be built on a raised platform as this one is. Very occasionally, people are tempted to add a false ceiling to the room below to accommodate the pipes, but unless the ceiling really is too high, take care about interfering with a room's natural proportions. The soil pipe for the toilet is a larger pipe, and, if you propose moving it, you may get protests from plumbers. However, it is almost always possible to move it; it may simply cost more to put it on a platform.

Having an open-plan bedroom-bathroom often means that you can treat yourself to the luxury of a giant bath. What is not apparent here – because it stands in a large area – is that this bath is also exceptionally large, another bonus gained from siting it centrally in a free-flowing space. The washbasin, too, is generously proportioned and is in an antique design so that it sits stylishly with the bath and bedframe.

If you have a central bath, remember to include somewhere to stand a soap dish or shampoo bottles when you are in the bath. This bath is boxed in and this has created a wide enough rim around it for such practicalities, but many free-standing roll-top baths don't have the kind of edge you could balance a bottle on. You will need either to build in a shelf nearby or have a table to hand. Similarly, make sure that the towel rail is within easy reach – you don't want to walk across the room dripping with water.

lighting and safety

Careful consideration must be given to lighting and electrical equipment anywhere near water, and most countries have regulations that cover the kind of lamps or sockets that can be used within reach of a bath or basin. Electricity and water are, truly, a lethal combination, and you should never take risks, especially when there are children about. While some people do bend the rules a bit, it is wise to do so with the utmost of caution. For example, it would be very dangerous indeed to have any piece of electrical equipment, such as a lamp or a hairdryer, so near to either the bath or basin that it might fall in. This would electrocute you. This means that you should not have side tables with lamps or standard lamps anywhere near the bath area. In this room the only lighting comes from wall lights, and lamps are right across the other side of the room on the bedside tables. Even wall lights should be sealed – there are an increasing number of good bathroom light designs now available on the market – and you should not be able to change a bulb while standing in the bath! Any sockets in this part of the room should be the kind of bathroom sockets specifically designed for use with an electric razor.

storage

An extensive and well-planned storage system is the key to the serenity of this bedroom. There is a place for everything, and everything is in its place. Two whole walls of cupboards have been

1: Cupboard doors open to reveal shelves.

2: The radiators are below the window seat, allowing the heat to spread out into the room rather than being lost through the window.

above right: Wooden flooring works well for bathrooms or bedrooms. Vinyls, linoleum and some carpets are also suitable for a bedroom-bathroom.

designed to fit in unobtrusively without dominating the room. One wall of cupboards was actually built in the adjacent spare bedroom, with the doors knocked out of the wall between the two rooms and opening into the main bedroom. This involved moving the door to the spare bedroom slightly further along the landing, which was not a difficult job.

The other wall of drawers and cupboards was built around the windows, offering the opportunity for a window seat, and making the windows look attractively deepset. There is a gentle slope at the window edge of each cupboard, making the windows look larger and the window seats more comfortable. The radiators could have posed a problem, but long low ones were installed under the window seats.

BED/BATH: ALL IN ONE CHECKLIST

■ Bathroom areas should not have ordinary sockets, and lighting should be approved bathroom lighting, flush against the wall or ceiling and sealed. Only bathroom shaver sockets can be used, and it should never be possible to change a lightbulb when standing in the bath. Also make sure that no one can use hair dryers or other types of electrical equipment in the bathroom area for safety reasons.

■ If you regularly open windows and doors, then you may not wish to use an extractor fan, but it can be useful during the winter months. Bedroom-bathrooms will be bigger than most standard bathrooms so you may need to check with a retailer if you need a more powerful fan.

■ Check that towels are within easy reach, and also that there is a suitable surface near the bath for shampoo bottles, soap and other accessories.

■ A bath positioned centrally in the room is not suitable for a shower, except one that is hand-held.

the bedroom/ playroom

This bedroom/playroom was designed by James Lynch of City Lofts for a family that has four children, ranging from a small baby to a ten-year-old. By building in a series of different pieces in one coordinated design, he has created a private, lockable desk zone for the eldest child, plus flexible sleeping platforms, lots of storage, open playing space and the option for the area to evolve as the children grow up.

A top sleeping platform runs the length of this bedroom/playroom and can take two or three mattresses. Below is a built-in cot, which can convert to a desk area later on. There is also a playing space that can ultimately house pull-out wardrobes when the need for more storage space grows, and (inset) a third bed platform.

built-in growth

The starting point for this design was to provide sleeping and playing space for four young children whose needs will change as they grow up. At first glance, you might expect free-standing furniture to be more flexible than a built-in design, but this series of platform beds, desks and storage units will adapt to suit their needs and carry them well into their teens.

The flexibility starts with wide sleeping platforms that run the length of the room on either side rather than conventional bunk beds. There is enough space on both sides for extra mattresses to be added if a friend spends the night, and, when the spare mattress is removed the platform space can be used for playing. Traditional bunk beds are often quite restrictive, and it can be difficult for an adult to sit up and read to a child. With these platforms there is plenty of room to sit up on both levels, making the extra space useful for board games or model-building – in fact anything that needs to be kept out of the way of the curious fingers of toddlers or the irritating interference of inquisitive younger children.

The platforms also make better use of the space underneath than ordinary bunk beds. Along one side of the room – where the

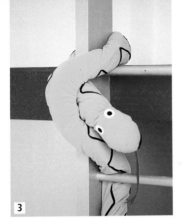

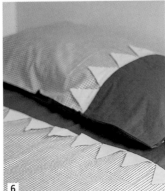

1: The built-in cot has scope to be turned into either a seating area or a second desk zone when the baby grows out of it.

2: The ladder up to the top sleeping platform helps to evoke the era of pirate ships.

3: The bright colours of the room echo the children's toys.

4: Extra storage is slotted in whenever possible.

5: Bulkhead lighting offers individual pools of light.

6: Brightly coloured bedlinen adds to the decorative scheme.

eldest child sleeps – there is a long, simple desk-worktop where homework can be done or games can be played. A long sliding door with portholes in it for the light can be slid across and locked, thus keeping this space sacrosanct from the meddling of the younger ones. In this way, the child who has almost reached his teens already is given his own space, while still sharing a room with his brothers and sisters. The desk is one long strip of kitchen work surface – in this case a recycled plastic from Made of Waste, which is not only cheaper than the equivalent length of wood, but also tougher and easier to clean. Underneath the desk surface there is room for filing cabinets or more shelving as the need arises, and another chair can be added if two or more children want to work there together. On the other side, where the top platform is longer and will eventually house two mattresses – even three when friends come to stay – the area below is used for a built-in cot, an empty space, and a third, single-platform for

FLOOR PLAN
(1) Sleeping platform for oldest child with desk below. (2) Partition to window with holes for light. (3) Window running the width of the room. (4) Extra storage tower. (5) Sleeping platform above built-in cot. (6) Sleeping platform continues over play space. (7) Sleeping platform over lower sleeping platform.

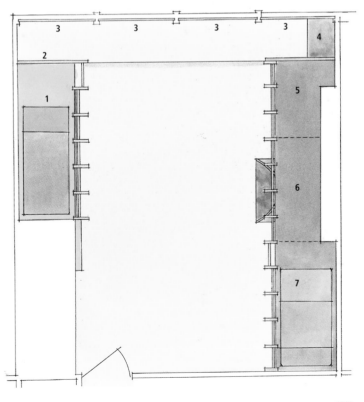

■ Adults protest at children's untidy rooms, yet often fail to provide the storage facilities needed to keep the room tidy. Children's rooms need more comprehensive storage than adults', not less.

■ Don't fob off a child with second-rate furniture, such as drawers that stick or unattractive pieces that have been rejected as sub-standard by the rest of the house.

■ Reassess living and storage needs once a year. The quantity and style of toys and clothes change as the children grow up. Think of sports kit and school uniform, hobbies, computers and homework, and recreational books.

■ If you start out with a romantic scheme for a small baby, be prepared to redecorate within five years, as he or she may outgrow it.

■Try to provide an extra bed – anything from a pull-out mattress to a sofabed. A parent may want to sleep in the same room as a small baby from time to time, and older children usually enjoy having friends for sleepovers.

the toddler, who cannot safely sleep up top yet. When the baby leaves the cot, the toddler will be old enough to sleep on the upper levels, and the baby will take his position on the lower sleeping platform. Below both the cot and the lower platform, there are pull-out storage boxes set on wheels for toys and clothes, and these will be turned into drawers eventually when the children's toys become less bulky and they need more storage space for clothes.

storage and light

The built-in cot also has storage beneath it, and when the baby outgrows it, the rails will simply be removed, thus eliminating all evidence that it was ever a cot. With the base kept in its current position, this will turn into a little built-in sofa or bench seating. But there is also the option to raise the base to create an additional desk area, which will be useful in the future when two or even three of the children will have school homework and revision to do.

1: One long sleeping platform has room for an extra mattress for a friend, while below is a long desk area with filing cabinets.

2: The 'porthole' doors slide closed and can be locked.

3: There is plenty of room for books and games on the shelves above and the cabinets below the desk.

88

The large windows run the whole width of the room, so the end pieces – the equivalent of the foot of a bed – stop just short of the windows. Portholes are cut in the left-hand end piece, to add light to the eldest child's desk area, while the right-hand side is used for a tall series of shelves which currently hold more boxes of toys. In future these can also be used as bookcases, display cases for models or shelves for storing videos, CDs and other equipment. The long raised platform at the window acts either as a window seat or an extra level for toys and games.

In between the built-in cot and the lowest platform bed is an empty space, which is now used for playing. It gives the children the option of putting up a tent or playing at theatre. However, as they grow up tents will be less important and storing school clothes and games equipment will be a problem. The design for the room includes adding three pull-out wardrobes in this area to increase storage. As the depth of the platform is greater than a wardrobe needs to be, the most effective way of maximizing hanging space is to have deep narrow wardrobes, that pull out on casters very much as some kitchen larder units do, rather than having a conventional wardrobe system with opening doors.

Keeping all the practical elements to either side of the room makes the most of the play area in the centre, which is important. Also, with open storage easy to hand, tidying up can be done quickly, so it is easy to persuade the children to do it.

Decorating an area for four different personalities is always going to be difficult. Originally, the eldest boy wanted a spaceship theme, while the younger ones begged for a pirate ship. Even in a biggish room, this would have looked chaotic and untidy, so compromises were made by using blocks of colour to create a semi-industrial look – which appealed to all the children.

The circular holes are spaceship-like, and the ladders up to the platforms could be thought to be the rigging of a pirate ship. But they all work together under the industrial theme that has been created. Blue was eventually chosen as the main colour, because it is a relatively calm and peaceful theme for a bedroom, and the bright splashes of red and yellow are testament to its extra function as a place for some play.

4: A theme of primary colours works for books, toys and bedlinen alike.

5: There is plenty of room for playful activities in this room.

6: Many of the toys are decorative in their own right.

7: Bed platforms are supported by wooden end pieces just short of the window. This leaves a space for a bookcase, creating useful extra storage.

bed/bath: screened off

A bedroom and bathroom divided by a screen, rather than a wall, has many of the advantages of an open-plan space without loss of privacy. There will be more light, and a spacious feel in the room. Here designer and cookery writer, Alastair Hendy, has used a wooden block as a room divider-cum-headboard, allowing light to flood in from the bathroom to the bedroom, and letting the bathroom's blue mosaics become a colour feature in an otherwise neutrals-and-naturals bedroom.

A washbasin hangs on the other side of this giant block of wood, which also serves as a headboard. A bath, too, is virtually hidden from sight, but a reclaimed 1930s' shower head and radiators (inset) can be seen from the bedroom area .

creating light

This is a very contemporary interior, but such a layout would work equally well in more traditional materials and designs, and it's an idea that can offer a real alternative to a boxy en-suite bathroom or a completely open-plan look. One of the biggest problems about carving a bathroom out of a bedroom is the effect on the windows, and the relationship of the windows to the shape of the room both before and afterwards. Here the bathroom receives almost all the natural light available to the room – apart from some borrowed light from an adjacent room via a glass brick wall – so a screen or an open-plan arrangement was essential. Even in a more conventional space the same problems may exist. For example, placing the bathroom away from the windows restricts how you place the bed, and this is when it is well worth considering using a solid, but incomplete

FLOORPLAN
(1) Storage cupboard hidden by floor to ceiling panel. (2) Similar walk-in airing cupboard/utility area. (3) WC. (4) Storage chest. (5) Bed. (6) Partition. (7) Washbasin. (8) Bath. (9) Shower.

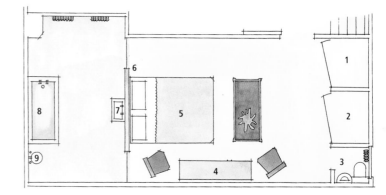

1 and 2: The ultra-modern look of the bed, situated on its platform, works very well with the sleek, smooth lines of the 1930s' furniture.

3: Full length floor-to-ceiling panels are doors with invisible press catches. They lead to a toilet, walk-in wardrobe and laundry area.

1

2

screen. It does not have to reach the ceiling – anything just over the height of a tall man will conceal everything proportionately.

There are several other good tricks in this bedroom-bathroom, any one of which could be adopted in other rooms. One wall appears to be three large panels – in fact, they are three floor-to-ceiling flush doors, each of which presses open. One conceals the toilet. Another leads into a walk-in closet with a washing machine, tumble-drier and other equipment. The third is a closet with shelves. These three large 'cupboards' mean that furniture in this room is minimal. Just one giant chest has pride of place.

With a bathroom area that is partially on view, there needs to be a sense of visual discipline about the way it is fitted out. Here the theme of a 1930s' lido successfully links the building's historic past with its current contemporary interpretation, as 1930s' design has much in common with the clean, sweeping lines of today's modernism.

4: Drawers double up as steps that lead to the sleeping/ storage platform.

5: A wall of glass bricks helps to bring some extra light into the bedroom from the stairwell area.

- If using architectural salvage, remember that the cost of renovation can be as nuch as double or treble what you have paid for the item in the first place. Refer to page 149 for information on specialist craftsmen and organisations.

- The weathered or aged look is part of the charm of recycled items for many people, but check the functionality carefully.

- Spare parts are often a problem if, say, tap sizes have changed over the decades. You may able to improvise – for example, tap washers are no longer made for these taps but a piece of rubber, cut to size, works just as well.

- If renovation worries you, many companies are making exactly the same designs today. You may be able to buy identical models that are new. However, many of the 'Victorian-style' or 'Georgian-style' items available in large DIY shops are often cheap pastiches and best avoided if you want authenticity.

To maintain a clear view of a straight floor from the bedroom, the standard shower tray was dispensed with, so water pumps from the giant showerhead onto the mosaic floor. This large showerhead – a genuine antique refitted for current plumbing – pumps out an enormous volume of water at any one time. This means that the drainage must be carefully assessed. Without a shower tray, it's necessary to have the tiled floor at a slope towards the drain or the bedroom may be flooded. And even with a shower tray, you can get flooding unless there is good drainage.

The bath was made of concrete breeze blocks, sealed to keep water out, and tiled in the same blue mosaic tiles as the rest of the room. Always check how slippery bathroom floor tiles are before buying.

visual links

Many fittings, such as taps, basins and radiators, are recycled from architectural salvage yards and renovated. This can prove tricky as it can be difficult to get the right washers for antique taps, for example. In this case, the owner cut rubber washers himself, but it is usually difficult to get plumbers to agree to this. There are many professional companies that renovate salvage items such as radiators and parquet flooring (see directory), but do remember that this can add about one third to the cost. Slabs of marble or marble tiles, for example, can be restored by cleaning and polishing.

far right: The sloping glass roof is the only natural light available to this bedroom/bathroom, as it is situated in a basement.

1 and 2: Washers for these taps are no longer made, but a piece of rubber, that has been cut to fit, works just as well.

3: Square, simple lines and a minimum of decorative detail keep this bathroom area looking contemporary. The giant showerhead is a reclaimed model from the 1930s. The bath is concrete breeze blocks, sealed to hold water, and then tiled with the same mosaic tiles that decorate the floor and the ceiling area.

4: The taps and basin are also reclaimed architectural salvage items.

5: The toilet is hidden away neatly behind the giant door panels on the other side of the room, and is a contemporary model.

1

2

colour

fragrance

storage on wheels

freestanding mirrors

hatboxes and bandboxes

Storage is the key to style and comfort. Displaying items on hangers makes them easier to find, while concealing them in boxes and drawers reduces clutter. Most bedrooms-plus benefit from a mixture of the two, but all require a place for everything to fit everything in its place.

innovative shapes

flexible furniture

seat-cum-linen basket

box storage

Use the walls: take radiators up rather than along, divide up hanging space into short and long, try out flexible hanging shelves, and hang shoes, ties, scarves and belts. Look out for multiple hangers that take several sets of trousers, blouses, folding items, and even collapsible hanging wardrobes.

ideas for hanging

designer linoleum

dynamic towel rails

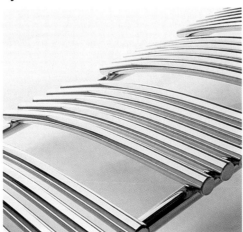

armchair to relax in

coloured glycerine soaps

bedside lighting

In the bedroom comfort and functional excellence must be balanced because a good night's sleep is as important as a healthy diet. A well designed bed is one that offers perfect rest as well as useful extras. Check out the soft elements: chairs, blankets, bedlinen – these are the definers of luxury.

beautiful bedlinen

cosy blankets

sheer comfort

innovative furniture

chests of drawers

drawers for bulky items

storage on wheels

Chests of drawers can be large or small, portable or fixed, antique or contemporary, but varying sizes and shapes of drawers are useful. Bathroom storage is essential to reduce clutter – either borrowed from other parts of the house or purpose-designed for the bathroom.

compartment storage

bathroom storage

VERTICAL

LIVING

You can often carve valuable extra living space out of a house if you think vertically. Halls and stairways, basements and mezzanine areas could all be used for storage, shower rooms, toilets, sitting or relaxing areas, or sites for home offices. Bookcases, for example, built just the width of a book, can be positioned along the narrowest of corridors or down a slender space such as around a door or under a window. And don't forget the roof – either open it up for double height rooms or fit cupboards and hatches for long-term storage.

Although the spaces are small, it is worth taking the extra time, trouble and, if necessary, spending extra money to ensure that they are exactly right. When centimetres count, you can't afford mistakes: check measurements, act out movements within the space (for example, to check whether a tall person can stand or reach easily) and make sure you understand exactly what the result will be.

the understairs/ office

This compact home office makes maximum use of the space under the stairs that is often forgotten or treated as a glory hole. Instead of a stair rail, there are shelves reaching from floor to ceiling (inset), allowing light in from the floor above. A comprehensive storage system is tucked into the stair treads at several levels from low cupboards at the base to eye-level shelving. A vibrant colour scheme based on ochre and blue adds warmth to the area.

Using open shelving against the stairs instead of a bannister maximizes the use of vertical space. Here, these shelves are open to either the stairs or the hallway, but they could also be backed with toughened or frosted glass, or coloured Perspex without cutting out light.

Defining the space

Every part of this area under the stairs has been used to its maximum capacity in a design by architect Melissa Merryweather. It is an exceptionally tight corner to work in, which meant that careful – and absolutely accurate – plans were critical, with every aspect worked out finely to the last measurement before any structural work took place. Such a task is easier if the stairs are being built or re-built at the time, as the steps and the rise can be made to work with the design, but this is not essential.

Firstly, establish what you need in terms of head height and reach. It is completely impossible to work in an area if you hit your head on a stair tread every time you lean forward. It is also important to feel sure that you'll be happy with the way the stairs slope overhead, and that you won't find it claustrophobic.

Then list everything you plan to do in the office, and how long you plan to spend there at any one time. This one is both a home office and a 'command control centre' for the house, containing all the domestic bills and papers as well as work. It is used for an estimated 4–8 hours a week, although no-one spends more than an hour or so at a time at the desk. This establishes where compromises can be made. In such a confined space, for example,

it is not possible to have a full desk surface and an ergonomically correct office chair with a back, but, because it will only be used for short periods a space-saving stool can be substituted instead, to leave a relatively generous desk area.

There could be no compromises on storage, however, and by measuring the wall and stair space accurately it was possible to pack a surprising number of boxes and baskets into a very small area. There needed to be a gap for feet, knees and legs under the main part of the desk, but there was room for storage at the side. Big A4 boxes are set on the floor with a shelf for document boxes above. At eye level above the desk there is a shelf for A4 files, while below, where the stair treads recede, are two open shelves and a deep cupboard for general items such as stationery and record books. There is room for a few more files, plus CD Rom and disc boxes on the desk top and the shelves by the staircase.

1: Neatly labelled box files are ideal storage in a small space. Choose different coloured ones for easy identification.

2: This shelving is structurally supporting the room above, and would normally be a solid wall, making the hall darker.

FLOORPLAN
(1) Stool. (2) Desk area.
(3) Files on the shelves and in the cupboard, built into the stair treads. (4) Telephone area. (5) Area for the computer. (6) Box files on top of desk area, with two extra shelves of storage situated beneath. (7) Open shelving that replaced stair bannisters. (8) Stairs to room up above.

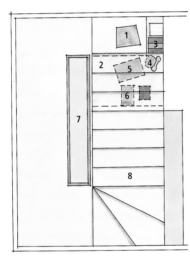

Light is a major issue in small, awkward spaces such as this. Some element of natural light is essential, and if even the tiniest window can be carved out of the wall, then this will make a great deal of difference. Otherwise use 'borrowed' light, such as here where the daylight streams in from the roof lights above the staircase. Most halls and stairways have some access to sunlight. Good electric lighting is essential too – low-voltage halogen spotlights equate most closely to natural daylight, and, as there may not be room for a desk lamp, check that the spotlights can angle light where you will need it without reflecting unduly on the computer screen. Fire precautions are important in halls and stairways, so the spotlights shown here are in fireproof housing, and wherever possible fireproof materials have been used.

Understairs spaces are also very much on view to everyone passing through the house, so here a deliberate policy has been made to use warm, strong colours in a palette of ochre, grey and blue. It is well worth investing in some stylish storage boxes and files, or at least coordinating them.

3: The deep cupboard is fitted into the stair treads. Note the low-voltage halogen lightbulb set in to the tread above.

4, 5 and 6: Shelves at different heights can maximize storage: vases and bottles for the living area can be housed above.

THE UNDERSTAIRS/ OFFICE CHECKLIST

■ There is no room for mistakes. Take yourself through a day at the desk, and make sure you would be comfortable. Measure out all your actions. For example, sitting at the desk, leaning forward and standing up. Check your head room and elbow room against the stair tread and the walls.

■ Measure the space you need for desk, storage and chair. Can you get them all in? Where can you compromise? If you intend to work long hours, you will need an adjustable office chair with good back support. It should be on casters and be able to swivel.

■ Have power points put in for a computer, fax, printer and telephone. Do not rely on an extension cable from a hall socket, because trailing wires are dangerous.

■ Fit good lighting. All electrical equipment should be fire-proofed.

■ Measure the space for shelves and storage accurately. Allow for large and small boxes, using the full height and width of available wall space as a grid.

105

the mezzanine/ living space

The principal difficulty with converting basements is that there is often little access to natural light ad they were originally designed for storage rather than living. This apartment – converted by cookery writer and designer Alastair Hendy from an old printing factory – is a prime example. By cutting out a 'well' area, light was borrowed from the floor-to-ceiling windows on the ground floor, opening up the space and illuminating beautifully the stylish open-plan kitchen beneath.

A narrow mezzanine walkway leading to an open staircase provides access to the kitchen level. For those working in the kitchen (inset) this means a double-height space, while there is a warren of cupboards that provide some useful storage in the darker areas to the side of the room.

creative planning

The owner, cookery writer and designer, Alastair Hendy, decided to sacrifice part of the ground floor in order to open up the whole of the basement. He cut a hole in the floor, with access via a mezzanine walkway and stairs. This meant light could stream in from the floor-to-ceiling windows on the ground floor, and, by changing the panes of the narrow slit to match these windows, he was able to make it appear all part of one long light source. This created a security problem as windows at ground or basement level are vulnerable to being broken – so he installed a metal grille, similar to those used in shops and businesses. This slides down at the touch of a button to provide privacy or security.

The result of enlarging the window and removing part of the floor is a kitchen with a double-height ceiling in its working and eating area. This well is large and bright, and throws light onto storage and cooking areas at the sides which have their original ceilings. This trick of removing part of a floor could also make a basement with a low ceiling a viable living space. A cut-out well is worth considering in many instances – it may sacrifice more of the floor above, but it can create a really good, light working area.

The light well also offered the option of creating a second room – a bedroom-bathroom (see pages 94–99) with light 'borrowed' from this well, using a wall of glass bricks between the kitchen and the bedroom. In these rooms he also used another device for increasing the light. At one side there was an area where the basement extended further to the side of the building than the walls of the ground floor, and by roofing this extra space with translucent (not transparent) glass, light pours in from overhead. Overhead light is always the most effective – a small overhead hatch window will give as much light as a larger side window. Sometimes it's possible to extend a basement area out into the garden, and with a glass roof you'll get a light open room.

By sinking the kitchen down into the open well, this masks it off from the main living room, and makes it less than open-plan, but accessible. This means that the relaxing/living zone upstairs is free from the sight of cooking clutter, although from the mezzanine walkway both rooms can be seen. This demands strong visual links, such as using professional catering materials in both areas, bold, big pieces of furniture and a minimalist use of colour in this case.

3

4

1

2

1: A contemporary, industrial theme in tune with the building has been chosen to link the downstairs kitchen and upstairs living area.

2: The stairway down to the kitchen is simple and open.

FLOORPLAN
(1) Living area with sofas and fireplace. (2) Mezzanine platform. (3) Stairs down to kitchen. (4) Food preparation and sink. (5) Food preparation zone. (6) Range cooker. (7) Leading to storage under stairs.

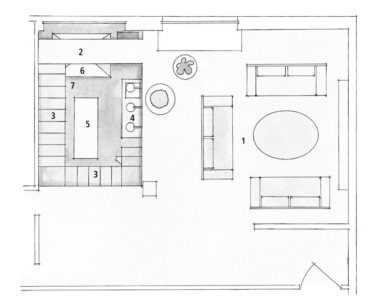

3, 4 and 5: The kitchen is effectively open-plan to the living room, but as it is on a level below the kitchen, clutter is concealed from the living area. These photographs show how the space was cut from the ground floor and how the mezzanine walkway and stairs curve round and down.

5

THE MEZZANINE/ LIVING SPACE CHECKLIST

■ Even a small amount of natural light will make a big difference to the success of a room. Try to create a 'well' somewhere, either by removing floor space from above, or by digging out towards the garden.

■ Light from above is more effective than side windows, so a small well or lantern light overhead will be as effective as a window four times the size.

■ Try to 'borrow' light when you divide the room up. Check out glass bricks or sandblasted glass partitions instead of solid walls.

■ Even the stairs will have some effect on light: metal rails will allow more to come through than a solid bannister.

■ Don't forget security – basement areas can be accessible and therefore vulnerable to burglars.

■ Check ventilation, damp-proofing and planning permission. Going ahead without first covering the formalities will cause problems when you try to sell.

the landing/ office

A great deal can be made of a small area in a hallway or on a landing. These slices of space – often left over from a more leisurely age when builders and houseowners could afford to be extravagant – can be just the right size to take a desk, chest or chair. The hallway usually offers a light well that affects the atmosphere of the whole house, so if you can make the space work without cutting out sunlight then you will create something usable that will leave your home feeling light and spacious.

A light, spacious corner of a hallway offers the opportunity for a useful home work zone that is used occasionally, rather than a full-scale office.

By organizing the desk and storage properly (inset), it is surprising how much you can fit in and also do in such a restricted space.

The desk is narrow enough to prevent the chair from constantly being in the way of people going up and down the stairs.

a basic office

This desk zone had been converted into a tiny bathroom by a previous tenant, and, by opening it up, the owners restored the light of a huge window to a first-floor landing. This kind of set up is for the person who only works at home intermittently – anyone trying to run a proper business from such a restricted area would soon feel frustrated. But for the person who just needs a staging post for bills and correspondence, or who has children who may want to use it for simple tasks like homework, it can take the pressure off other rooms in the house.

a quick, easy desk

It is unlikely that you will find exactly the right piece of furniture to fit in between the walls, but this doesn't have to mean commissioning anything complicated. For example, something as simple as a piece of wood or laminated ply, cut to measure then rested on filing cabinets or battens – or a combination of the two – will be both practical and inexpensive. Suppliers of kitchen

FLOORPLAN
(1) Window. (2) Desk. (3) Computer.
(4) Filing cabinet. (5) Chair. (6) Stairs.

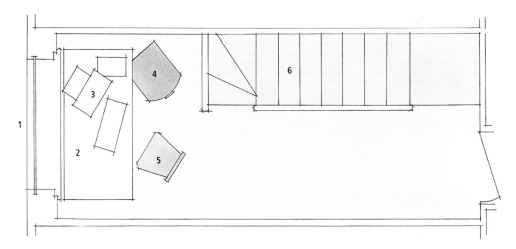

work surfaces are a good place to start, as you will need a fairly strong surface, and certainly one that won't warp or bend. Wood of the required thickness, such as beech, can be surprisingly inexpensive, or consider laminates – these are now available in a wide range of colours and finishes. If you're going to be using a personal computer at the desk, there are two things to bear in mind before ordering the surface. Firstly, make sure that the measurements you specify include the depth of the computer plus the keyboard. Secondly, remember that there is often quite a substantial amount of wiring to be taken into account. This should ideally run down the back of the desk, rather than trailing over your working surface, so you may want to have holes cut at the back, or simply leave a gap between the back of the work surface and the wall.

As people will be walking past this area every day, it's essential to make it look as good as possible. Plan all your storage carefully, and make sure that there is a box, basket or file for everything that you will need. Don't forget to include a wastepaper basket – it's a surprisingly simple thing but is very useful and can be only too easy to overlook.

1

2

1: Pretty boxes for mundane items such as stamps or large paper clips help keep the area looking good.

2: Bright light streams in onto the desk. This can cause glare on the computer, so it is best to fit a simple roller blind which goes neatly up and down rather than curtains. Constantly pulling curtains across would keep knocking things off the desk.

3: Keeping an informal colour scheme, such as all-brights, pastels or whites, for filing cabinets and furniture will help pull the work zone together. Incorporating a bright filing cabinet in an otherwise neutral scheme will only draw the eye unnecessarily and emphasize the clutter.

3

THE LANDING/OFFICE CHECKLIST

■ Make sure that chairs, corners of desks, tables or filing cabinets don't block the normal movement of people, especially when you're using the desk area. It is annoying, and potentially dangerous, to have a chair obstructing a corridor or hallway.

■ Even if the space is restricted it should be comfortable to work at. Areas to look at include desk height, chair height, the amount of work surface available and easy access to storage.

■ Make sure that all wires and plugs are out of sight and behind the desk. Trailing wires are dangerous, because they can trip people up, especially in parts of the house that they may be rushing through.

■ Keep decorative elements simple – this is not the place for elaborate curtains or fiddly displays of china, as things will get knocked over.

■ If you can't find a suitable desk, have wood or melamine blocks cut to fit and balance them on filing cabinets.

the landing/ sitting room

This sunny spot on the top floor of a small cottage is an open space that seems, at first sight, to be a serene and relaxing corner. In fact, it's a very hard-working area, providing extensive storage space for the nearby bedrooms and a mini-living room for those who want to get away from the pace of life in the rest of the house. A light well also successfully opens up what would otherwise have been a very small, boxy cottage.

Two bedrooms open directly into what was the main bedroom of the cottage. Now it is a peaceful sitting room (inset) lined almost invisibly with essential storage. Having the cupboards and chests of drawers on the landing helps to keep the bedrooms free and uncluttered.

115

an open space

This home was made from two small workers' cottages which have been knocked together. The original cottage had one main bedroom, which opened up directly from the stairs without any kind of wall or door as separation, and two tiny bedrooms leading off it. Its mirror image is on the other side, and there is a door cut into the wall to connect the two. Many owners might have walled this top area off to make a third bedroom, but the effect would have been to make the top floor feel dark and boxy. It seems a mad indulgence to leave it open-plan, but with extensive cupboards built discreetly into the walls and several chests of drawers, it offers plenty of storage space when left open-plan as well as making the atmosphere lighter and brighter. Having the drawers and cupboards just outside the two little bedrooms they serve also means that these can be kept clean and simple, with just a bed and side table as furnishings.

attention to detail

Both the cupboards and the door to the other side of the cottage are flush with the walls and have been kept as plain as possible, with spring-catches instead of handles, so they look like walls rather than cupboards. Every bit of space has been used, with smaller cupboards built under the eaves of the sloping roof, and varyingly graduated shelving ensures maximum capacity.

Cottage windows are often difficult to curtain, with their deepset, irregularly shaped areas. Here a simple scalloped pelmet, edged with braid follows the line of the window recess without being fussy. The primrose check design echoes the innocent rural charm of the cottage. A gentle creamy-white from Papers & Paints is in keeping with the age of the building as bright, brilliant whites were not invented until the 1920s. It also helps to maximize sunlight. The furnishings have been kept deliberately fresh and unpretentious too – it would not be appropriate to have expensive, over-the-top fabrics and fittings in a cottage that was built several hundred years ago for very humble inhabitants.

Checks and stripes against the rich patina of beautiful old wood create a look that is both timeless and contemporary. Another important point is that there aren't too many decorative elements. Apart from the white paint and the wood on the chair arms and on the chests, there is only the cheerful yellow and a collection of blue jars and pots. Too many colours or patterns fighting for space and air would have made the area less peaceful and harmonious.

Great attention to detail has been paid in this tiny area. The stair uprights, for example, have been specially cut to a design created by the owner, and the radiator is hidden by painted wooden slats with a small shelf above. The original beam in the ceiling has been left exposed to emphasize the slightly uneven lines of the cottage.

FLOORPLAN
(1) Storage cupboards.
(2) Window. (3) and (4) Pine
chests. (5) Chairs. (6) Table.
(7) Stairs. (8) Entrance.

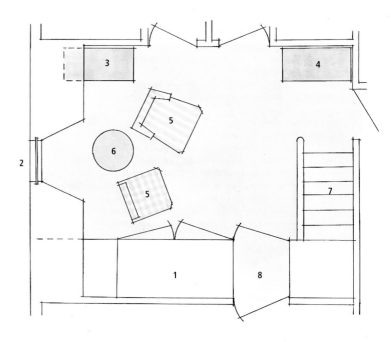

1

3

2

4

5

1 and 2: The cupboards are featureless and flush with the walls so they are completely unobtrusive.

3: Shelving is taken right under the eaves to make the most of the storage space in this old cottage.

4: A simple, cheerful window treatment and a slatted radiator cover are contemporary, but they also fit well with the overall cottage style.

5: A collection of blue and white Chinese jars is virtually the only decorative element in this understated colour scheme.

THE LANDING/SITTING ROOM CHECKLIST

■ If you want to keep storage discreet in living areas, keep decorative detail on cupboards and drawers to a bare minimum. Spring-catch doors, instead of handles, leave surfaces flush.

■ In a restricted space, fittings are highly noticeable. Bannisters, stair rails and radiator covers, for example, do not need to match, but it will make the space seem calmer if they work together decoratively.

■ Equally fabrics, curtain treatments and flooring will look less cluttered in a limited space if they follow a common theme.

■ Think about whether you want the furniture and fittings to link with your home's historical past or provide a contrast.

■ Pale or cheerful colours and white paint, with light floors, will make the space seem lighter and airier. Dark carpets or floorboards will darken a small space.

the staircase/ library

The stairs in this maisonette have been used for storage all the way. At the bottom, where they open out into the living room, drawers and cupboards have been installed to house an entire sound system, TV and associated equipment, while bookcases now replace bannisters as the stairs begin to rise. There is the optimum use of space, with every drawer, shelf and cupboard carefully planned and measured out to make sure that no usable area is wasted.

This bookcase replaces the previous bannister of the staircase entirely. It has been built with three different depths of shelves to take varying sizes of book. At its narrowest, the bookcase can store just paperbacks, but at the back it can take much larger volumes.

119

■ You can transform your house by organizing the storage of books, tapes, CDs, magazines, videos and tapes properly.

■ To avoid losing any floor space in your home, look at where shelves can be built in. These take up less room than freestanding bookcases or cupboards and can be fitted into surprisingly small corners or narrow corridors.

■ Measure up shelf and cupboard heights accurately, taking into account the size of big books (for example, illustrated coffee-table books), smaller books and paperbacks.

■ Avoid having deep cupboards where you have to search for things. If a space is deep (for example, under a flight of stairs) build drawers that can be pulled out for easy access. Even a tiny drawer could take a couple of dozen tapes or a store of back-up computer disks.

utilizing space

The key to the success of this design was to measure up everything accurately. There are pull-out drawers that are exactly the right size for videos or tapes, making it much easier to find them, rather than hunting around in the back of a cupboard, particularly considering the width of a stairway. The TV and music system have purpose-designed slots with holes drilled for the wiring, and the bookshelves have been measured to take three sizes of book – small paperbacks, large paperbacks and illustrated, coffee-table tomes. There is also some further shelf space for ornaments. To tie in with the rest of the room, it was painted in a shade of pale orange.

Using the space under the stairs for storage works best if it is carefully calculated. There is a piece of Japanese furniture called a *kaidan-dansu*, which is a chest of drawers built in a stepped fashion

1: Curves in the design of the bookcase give it a flowing, streamlined look and make it look less formal.

2: Cleverly designed, built-in storage under the stairs houses all the music and TV equipment.

3: Small drawers are very handy to have. They are easy to keep tidy, and they hold a surprisingly large amount of CDs and tapes.

FLOORPLAN
(1) Bookcase and storage under stairs. (2) Stairs.
(3) Bookcase on landing.

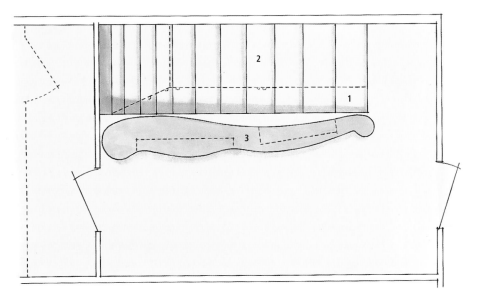

like stairs. It's a format that can offer helpful tips in Western design – try building drawers into the side of stairs, pulling out into the room. As the stairs rise, there is room for hanging things or tall objects, and you gain a great deal of extra storage by building varying sizes of cupboards to fit different sized objects. This is better than making one big cupboard or standard sizes of shelves and trying to store everything away haphazardly. Many people use this kind of understairs space for storing washing machines or microwaves, in which case you can build appropriate storage in the spare surrounding space to take all the necessary washing powder, ingredients or china.

extra storage

The same stairs have been used to increase the number of bookshelves, and these have been built in place of the bannisters. At the bottom of the bannister the shelves are just the width of a paperback book, plus a little extra, and there is access to them from the stair side. At the top, larger books can be accommodated – up to an A4 file size, and these can be reached from the landing.

The bookcase was made by cutting a curved piece of wood, with a central slot, and attaching it to the newel posts. A second piece of wood slotted into this, and shelves were screwed in between. A piece of kitchen worktop in beech made a broad top to the whole bookcase, and makes a useful staging post for laundry and other household items. This bookcase was then painted yellow to link it in with the bathroom upstairs and to contrast with a blue bedroom that leads off the upper landing.

Even the narrowest of halls and corridors can often be made to work harder by using such techniques, and books, in particular, take up very little space when stored vertically. One successful trick is to run a bookcase around a doorway – above it and on either side of it – so the door appears deepset. If the depth of the shelves is a bit more than a paperback book, the impact on floor space is negligible, yet many books can be accommodated.

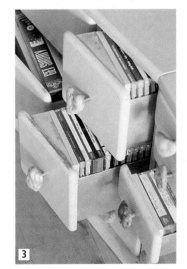

into the roof: kitchen/ living room

An attic space between the roof and the ceilings below can be more than just a place to store clutter. Removing the ceilings on the top floor, then carving a slice of vertical space out of part of the room, can be an exciting and practical way to create a stunning interior. Here a living room with a mezzanine kitchen makes a lively, light and easy-to-live-with double-use room.

A dining table overlooks the living area. It can be seen from below (inset) and is a sociable eating and working space, while also being separated enough to keep the clutter of cooking and eating out of sight. Extra light is provided by skylights, giving the room a sunny feel.

Innovative solutions

You will find houses with sloping roofs all over the world. The slice of space between the ceiling of the top floor and the roof is normally the storage area. Hundreds of unwanted items and bulky suitcases are shoved up there year after year, and usually forgotten. If there is enough space, an extra living floor may be possible, but very often there isn't quite enough head height to do this, and planning restrictions may mean that the outside roof level cannot be taken up. However, there are several ways of using the attic for something more exciting than a giant glory hole.

Firstly, consider what you can do if you remove the ceiling, exposing the roof to the room below. At the very least this will transform a humble bedroom with a low ceiling into a magnificent vaulted room. You may not be using that extra height for anything, but it will make the whole room feel more spacious.

Secondly, depending on how the stairs rise and what the layout of the top floor is, you may be able to use some of the full height space. This may not be as large as a whole room, but it could make a big difference to how the top floor works. A shower and a toilet carved out of ceiling space over a stairwell, for example, and reached by a short half-flight of stairs from the top floor, could make an extra bathroom without breaking up a bedroom.

If there is a little more space to work with, a mezzanine level can increase a house's floor area and add an extra useful 'room'. Here a mezzanine floor has been created along one side of the living room, leaving a double-height ceiling on the other side. This mezzanine is a kitchen, but it could also be a bedroom, dining or study platform. Had these two living spaces been walled off, they would have been strange boxy rooms. There is also the problem that most mezzanine areas, even if they are high enough for a tall man, do not legally have enough head height to be a proper room. As an all-in-one-space the area is sociable, spacious, light, and keeps the cooking and living areas separate but connected.

While adding an extra room or floor to a house often triggers off local planning problems, simply carving out a mezzanine in

the roof area is unlikely to require permission. This is because there is no change to the exterior of the house, although, in a few areas, you may need planning permission to add rooflights even if they're flush to the line of the roof. Otherwise the structural side is relatively straightforward, but do remember that hot air rises. In the winter this makes heating the extra high rooms easier, as heat will rise from the rest of the house, but you should talk to your builder about having an extra layer of insulation to prevent it from escaping altogether. In the summer, too, heat may be a problem. So make sure that there are several windows that will open to provide ventilation. When windows are in the roof, they are relatively secure, so if you like to leave them open often, choose a design that doesn't allow a rainstorm to drench your home!

This mezzanine formula works well with most designs. In this house white paint, white seating and simple painted wood create a fresh, airy feel and maximize the sunlight. Although it is in a busy city street, you could easily be by the sea or in the country.

left: The kitchen area is painted in soft colours to give it a living room feel. The original loft was almost definitely not high enough to stand up in, but by removing the ceiling and dropping the ceiling height on one side of the room, an extra half-floor is fitted in. It doesn't feel claustrophobic because of the double-height ceiling on the other side of the room.

right: White armchairs and polished floorboards maintain the simple, uncluttered atmosphere of the kitchen area.

FLOOR PLAN
(1) Living area. (2) Raised mezzanine for cooking/dining.
(3) Run of kitchen units.
(4) Dining table. (5) Bannister overlooking living area.

INTO THE ROOF: KITCHEN/LIVING ROOM CHECKLIST

■ Although simply removing ceilings is not difficult and shouldn't cause any structural problems, it is often a good idea to use an architect to plan the space properly.

■ Heating and ventilation are critical on a roof floor. Allow enough windows for a good flow-through of air, and an extra layer of insulation to prevent heat loss.

■ Windows that are flush to the roof, such as Velux, will let in more light than dormer windows. You may not be able to add dormer windows because of planning restraints.

■ Another excellent way of flooding the room with light is to replace a section of the roof with a 'conservatory' glass roof.

■ Don't neglect safety with mezzanine bannister rails. They should be secure enough for a baby or toddler not to fall through.

■ If you put a shower in this space you will need an extra pump. With a new toilet, take care with placing the soil pipe, as there are often restrictions on their location.

colour

stackable furniture

Small spaces can often benefit from large furniture. Choose chests for the optimum size of drawer – storage is often more effective when divided up into small manageable chunks. Sculptural, simple shapes in furniture prevent halls and mezzanines from looking cluttered.

different sized drawers

pedestal tables

ways of hiding technology

compact club-style chairs

space-saving stool

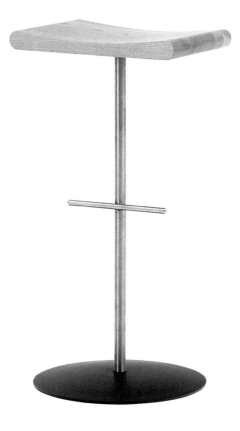

Time spent choosing exactly the right shape and size of furniture to make the most of an awkward corner will pay off in all areas, from chests and tables to chairs and radiators. The choice today is extensive – there are radiators for the narrowest strip of wall, and comfortable chairs for the most compact space.

special sizes of radiator

eye-catching flooring

127

hardwearing carpet

hanging shelving

Stairs and hallways feel more spacious when incorporated decoratively into the body of the house, while continuous colour and floor treatments create a feeling of flowing, open space. Even a few square feet of wall can house some extra shelves, split into compartments to keep items separate.

chevron stripes

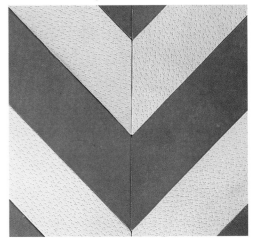

inspired design

foldaway furniture

extensive shelving

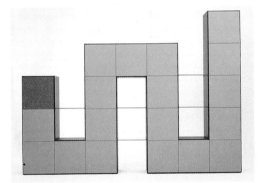

decorative shelving

Foldaway furniture, either fixed or free-standing, can turn a small corner into a room, and suspending items from walls frees up floor space. Halls and mezzanines are on display from most rooms in the house – simple shapes work well with decorative schemes elsewhere in the house.

simple shapes

CONSERVATORY

PLUS

Conservatories can either be all-year rooms – provided that they have double-glazing with good heating and ventilation – or summer-only rooms with less stringent requirements. They can be living or dining rooms, kitchens or corridors linking one part of a building to another, or you can replace part of a roof with conservatory glass to make a breathtaking room in the sky. Conservatories add extra floor space at ground level if part of the house wall is removed and supported with steel joists. They can fill the dead space between a house and its garden wall, or add an extra storey higher up.

Check several manufacturers or builders before committing yourself (using the tips on pages 134-137) and try to ensure that companies are both financially sound and experienced. To use the room properly, it is essential to plan the shape and the siting of the doors and windows carefully, so don't feel you have to accept a standard design.

country style: kitchen/dining/ conservatory

Adding a conservatory is often the best way of opening up dark or difficult rooms, or creating extra space for your household. This is a huge garden room-cum-kitchen, dining and living area. It allows the family to enjoy their country garden all year round, and has been planned as a versatile space with a cooking zone, a separate 'wet' area just off it, and all appliances, such as fridge, freezer and TV, are hidden inside custom-made cupboards from Smallbone of Devizes.

Natural materials – bare brick, beech flooring, granite work-tops – link the room with the garden in a contemporary way. The central island (inset) is a food preparation area, with its own sink. The cooking range is behind the pillars and the doorway leads to a small, washing up and storage area.

a flexible space

This is a large room, but it still needs careful planning. The temptation in bigger kitchens is to spread everything out, and this usually results in a room that is both exhausting to work in and lacks flexibility. Here all the cooking is done in approximately one quarter of the space, and there is literally one step from the food preparation area to the cooking range, and three steps to the washing-up and china storage area. This not only makes life much easier for the cook, but also leaves the maximum amount of space free in the rest of the room for playing, dining or large parties.

The central island is not, in fact, central, but is set to one side. It is the food preparation zone, with a granite worktop, giant chopping board, rubbish disposal, a sink for rinsing, washing and adding water, and a breakfast bar with stools. Just beside it is a handsome larder cupboard designed and custom-made, which houses the fridge, microwave and television. Keeping all these elements hidden gives it much more of a living room feel.

The main sink, along with the dishwasher and all the storage for glass, china and cutlery is in a small alcove off the main room – what would previously have been called a 'butler's pantry'. This convenient arrangement hides dirty dishes or pans awaiting washing from sight, and also means that the person washing up and the cook need not get on each other's toes. Most importantly, it means that unloading the dishwasher or putting things away after drying them on the draining board requires no more than opening a cupboard and stretching out an arm.

an all-year room

Building a conservatory that will really be an all-year room requires planning and investment. Too many conservatories are merely glass houses tacked onto the sides of buildings, with inadequate heating and ventilation. These issues are critical, or you will waste your money. While it is more expensive to build a conservatory properly, it is very good value for money if it adds another room to your house or makes your current space more

Having the sink, dishwasher, glass storage and china cupboards all together in the 'wet area' off the main conservatory cuts down on walking around an otherwise large room.

FLOORPLAN
(1) Doors from sitting room.
(2) Dining table. (3) Central
island. (4) Extra sink, waste
disposal and chopping board.
(5) Aga and hob. (6) Wet area
off main conservatory.
(7) Main sink. (8) Dishwasher.
(9) Cupboards for glass and
china. (10) Armoire for fridge,
television and dry food
storage. (11) Doors to garden.

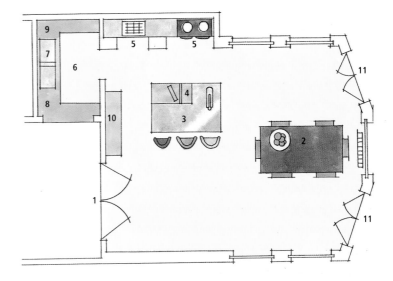

1 and 2: Custom-made
wooden cupboards in a
contemporary style neatly
house all the kitchen
paraphernalia and appliances,
such as the microwave.

3, 4 and 5: To soften the sleek
look of the modern kitchen
equipment, it has been fitted
next to or built into natural
time-honoured materials such
as granite, brick or wood.

■ Buy a good quality construction for your conservatory. Don't just buy a standard package without checking that it offers all that's needed: double glazing and toughened glass is essential for heating/security reasons. Polycarbonate roofs are cheaper, but brittle, noisier and opaque. Double-glazed roofs are more expensive, but can be repaired and look better.

■ Ventilation is the key: you need to be able to open several windows in the roof plus one-third of the side windows. Side opening windows are better than top-hanging ones.

■ Consider the effect of the shape on usable space. Rectangles and squares offer more space and flexibility. Bay-shaped conservatories limit furniture placement.

■ Draw a scale map of the conservatory and furniture, and work out a room plan before finalising the design.

■ Central doors cut down usable space. Try using side doors instead.

usable. Conversely you may waste what is still quite a large sum of money if you buy a cheap conservatory, and only use it for a few weeks a year.

There are, essentially two kinds of conservatories. One is a self-contained room on the back or side of the house, with the original doorway to the garden maintained as a door between house and conservatory. The second is when part of the back or side wall of a room is removed and the conservatory is added to make an existing room, such as a kitchen, larger and lighter. Either can work well, but it's worth thinking about exactly which would suit you better. This conservatory/kitchen/dining room is the latter, thus creating a large free-flowing space. This is also a technique that works excellently on a much smaller scale: a small, dark kitchen can be completely transformed by removing one wall and replacing it with even a small 3m (10ft) conservatory.

Secondly, look at several different plans before you agree on a shape. It may sound premature to say that you should know where every piece of furniture will go before the first brick is laid, but it is the only way to ensure that you get what you want. Make a simple scale plan of the conservatory – drawing it as 300mm = 25mm (1ft = 1in) for example – and then cut out scaled-down pieces of paper to show furniture (such as your dining table, side tables, armchairs or sofa). Use these to try out a few different room layouts, and see how flexible the room will be. A point to note is that a bay shape gives you less wall space than rectangular or square conservatories, so that if you choose a bay shape your only option may be a small table in the centre. It's also worth considering the position of the door. If it is straight ahead, then people going out to the garden will cut across living space. It may be better to have a side door. Discuss these issues with your conservatory designer, bearing in mind that you're the one who's going to live in the house, and if they just want to sell you their standard package, you may get better value elsewhere.

Next, consider the structure. Double glazing (using toughened glass) is essential if you want to use the room all year round, and, if you have opened up the wall to the house, it will also make the conservatory as secure as any other room in the house.

above: There's no need to use 'conservatory' furniture – your home will be more flexible if tables and chairs can also be used elsewhere in the house.

below: In a room designed in a sleek, contemporary style, a few more exuberant touches, such as fitting a candelabra, can look especially good.

If the conservatory is north facing, the glass should also be 'low-e' or 'low emissivity', which reflects heat back into the room, but this isn't necessary if it is south facing. Your conservatory supplier should fit you with good window locks and a five-point lock (as with front doors) for the doors to the garden.

The roof can either be made of poly-carbonate or double-glazed glass. Poly-carbonate is much cheaper, but it is opaque, very noisy in the rain, and eventually goes brittle (after about 10 years), when it can't be repaired. Double glazing looks better, is less noisy and, provided the wood has been properly treated, will last longer. If panes of glass do crack, they can also be repaired, so the structure will last a lifetime or more. Opt for safety glass, which has a film which will hold the glass in place if it breaks (this is rare, but a tree may lose branches in a major storm.). The roof should have at least 15° of slope, or you will get weather damage. If you can't manage that (because of windows, for example), have a flat bitumen roof with a roof lantern in the centre.

Conservatories can be made of softwoods, or non-endangered hardwoods. Agbar, for example, is a hardwood that is approved by Friends of The Earth. Ideally use hardwoods because they don't contract and expand as much as softwoods, and the extremes of heat and cold in a conservatory can be more than normal. Softwoods can be treated to make them more suitable.

Ventilation is absolutely critical to a comfortable conservatory. You should be able to open several roof hatches (depending on the size of the roof) and at least one-third of the side windows should be openable. Side opening windows give better ventilation than top hanging ones.

Once you have the double glazing and ventilation sorted out, then heating is straightforward and you should be able to add radiators onto your central heating system. Underfloor heating is comfortable, especially with tiles, stone or wood flooring, but it may demand more piping than your heating system can maintain.

When it comes to furnishing a conservatory, you don't need to have 'garden furniture'. As this shows, any furniture made of natural materials looks good. And if you're short of space, then you'll want furniture that can be used elsewhere in the house.

right: This conservatory/kitchen/dining room links house and garden, contemporary and traditional, with the use of old brick and traditional window bars. Ivy provides some interesting, year-round greenery.

below: Wood, along with stone, terracotta or tiled floors are good choices for conservatories, but protect them with a good sealant.

city style: terrace/dining/ conservatory

A conservatory-dining room designed by Stephen Woodhams and Peter Romaniuk for the roof of a back extension transforms a maisonette in a busy street by giving it outside space for entertaining. An ingenious use of mirrors makes the narrow area, surrounded on three sides by walls, look larger than it is, and it is linked to the living zone (inset) by a decorative theme of metal, glass, wood and white.

Using the same materials (metal, glass and wood) to link the conservatory with the living room means that furniture can be switched easily between either area. Here the table looks equally good laid for a summer lunch in the conservatory or decorated with flowers in the main room.

outside

This maisonette situated above a shop is narrow and deep, and, with buildings on either side, it was originally quite dark. As there was no access to a garden, the owner, floral designer Stephen Woodhams, wanted to create an outside space for summer dining, with a small enclosed 'courtyard' on the remainder of the roof. Working with architect Peter Romaniuk, they designed a small conservatory to sit on top of the back extension of the shop below, opening up the kitchen area so that the space and air flows through all year round.

Siting a conservatory on a roof places great demands on the structure, and in this case the load weight was too heavy for the building to bear. The solution, devised by Romaniuk, was to fix the sheets of toughened glass to 12 steel beams. These beams are supported by the walls on either side, so that the weight of the conservatory is taken by both side walls as well as the roof, spreading the load. This has the added advantage of making the conservatory 'frameless' and lighter-looking.

The conservatory is drawn into the main room very simply by removing the window between it and the kitchen, and also by removing what had been a door onto the roof. This not only makes it easy to chat between the kitchen and the conservatory, but also improves the flow of air around the maisonette on hot days. This is a factor to consider if you're adding a hothouse space to the back of a building. As frameless conservatories are single-glazed only, they are rather less secure so metal security grilles are

The flooring (1, 2 and 3) combines a steel mesh, which allows lights to be set in underfoot, with metal 'factory floor' sheets. The sophisticated lighting system, plus a control for the doors, is operated by a panel of dimmer switches (4), including one that turns the glass doors from clear to opaque (far left). In this instance it operates merely as an experimental visual effect – the glass of the conservatory is clear on either side of it – but where privacy is an issue, it could be used in glass doors to abolish the need for curtains or blinds.

left: When adding a conservatory to a small space it is essential to have furniture that sits equally happily inside or out, as extra sets of tables and chairs will make the house feel more cramped. Here, these dining chairs and table are also used inside, but when they are in the conservatory the main room feels much more open and spacious.

extended across the window and door, sliding right back and virtually invisible when not in use.

The other clever trick was to maximize light and space with giant mirrors on the two side walls of the conservatory. The steel sheets hang at an angle to the mirrored walls, leaving a narrow triangular strip for Stephen Woodhams' stunning floral designs, which are changed regularly each season. The mirrors and steel sheets obscure the edges of the conservatory, creating an illusion of an endless reflecting room, with the trapezoidal shape of the conservatory apparently expanded to seem almost like an octagonal room with several dining tables and plants.

This is a stylish urban space, so the metal, glass, wood and white theme transfers easily from inside to outside, with the metal-and-glass floor and table echoing the steel and glass structure.

CITY STYLE: TERRACE/DINING/ CONSERVATORY CHECKLIST

■ In small areas, a 'frameless' conservatory may look best. This is a contemporary style using toughened or laminated sheet glass bolted onto steel joists rather than a frame.

■ Best used in small space with an attractive view as there is no timber or brick to interrupt the eyeline. Larger conservatories need frames, as huge sheets of glass are too heavy.

■ Glass should be either toughened (shatters on breaking) or laminated (crazes or cracks but stays in place). Some people use a combination.

■ These conservatories are rarely double-glazed – it's too expensive and solid-looking.

■ Consult an architect on the positioning (eg whether it gets or needs direct sunlight). Check ventilation. Large doors here blow air through the door and window space at the back.

inside

The addition of the conservatory added about 25 per cent to the main living room, as well as making this area lighter and more flexible. The maisonette is in a fashionable part of town, where the cost of property is high, so every spare inch is a bonus. This main room functions as a kitchen, living room and, before the conservatory was added, also a dining area. The kitchen is at the back, and is the link between the conservatory and the main living area, while at the other end of the room are chairs, a sofa and a fireplace. The soft furnishings fit into the metal, glass, wood and white theme by being upholstered either in white or in fabrics and colours that evoke wood or metal: plain but handsome greys, plus shades of fawn, biscuit and honey that evoke natural timber.

The kitchen area is a tiny square at the back of the room, but still manages to house a large steel refrigerator, a big hob and oven, and masses of storage space. The priority was to design units that concealed the mess of food preparation and the sight of washing up, while allowing the cook to chat either to friends in the main room or join in the conservatory conversation. This is achieved by double-sided units: one side is higher and opens on

1: A wall of glass bricks separates the hallway from the kitchen in order to maximise light.

2: The metal sink faces out onto the conservatory, offering a chance to chat while preparing food or washing up.

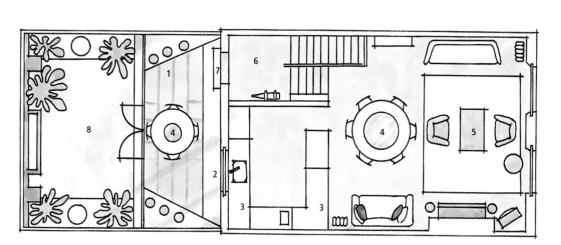

FLOORPLAN
(1) Sheets of toughened glass, bolted to hidden steel joists. (2) Former kitchen window, now removed to create an open hatchway and improve the air flow. (3) Kitchen units.
(4) Summer and winter positions for dining table. (5) Living area.
(6) Stairway connecting main room and conservatory to the other floor.
(7) Former door to stairway, now removed. (8) Outside balcony/terrace.

the living side, holding china and glass, while the other, with kitchen equipment, is lower and opens on the kitchen side. The work surface on this side is therefore hidden from view. Speakers for a stereo system, which are concealed on either side of the extractor fan, are insulated to give them the necessary protection from the heat. Hanging rails, to hold different types of cooking implements, and high level shelves for pans ensure that no space at all is wasted on the walls. Even the stairway is made to work hard as it contains a steel wine rack that runs right from the floor up to the ceiling.

above left: A high steel cupboard hides food preparation from the view of the diners, and the unit beside it opens onto both the kitchen and dining area.

above: The steel, wood and glass theme, even for pots and pans, prevents the cooking zone from looking cluttered.

'Paris café' chairs

collapsible fabric loungers

Folding furniture saves space and is easy to move around, while pieces that look equally good inside or outside offer the maximum flexibility, and also maintain the links between house and garden. Shapes and styles can be traditional or modern – remember that you don't have to be limited by conventional conservatory furniture.

relaxed, versatile tables and chairs

Shaker-style storage

circular table

Use texture as a visual link between inner and outer spaces. Natural materials or neutral finishes – such as wood, stone, metal and brick – will echo the colours and materials of the natural world outside, punctuated by brilliant splashes of colour inside or flowers outside.

metal and wood for lighter looks

stone or terracotta floors

vinyl and linoleum

Geometric patterns can be found in stone or terracotta flooring, created in vinyls or linoleum and in textured wool, sisal and seagrass. Textured or patterned flooring minimises the effect of muddy footsteps, providing a durable, hard-wearing and beautiful solution. Remember sunlight fades flooring in conservatories.

pendant lighting

seagrass, sisal, jute and wool

wirework pendants

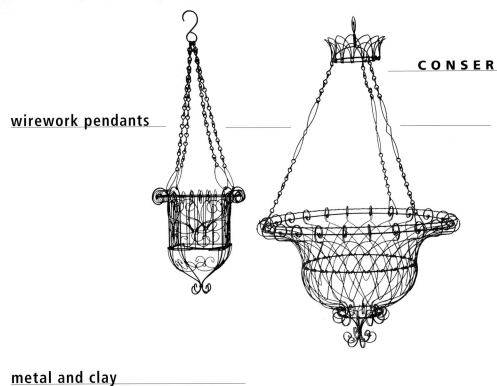

lantern lighting

metal and clay

Vertical shapes – pendant baskets, pots, candles, lanterns and lights – define the space. Repetition – two baskets, three candles, four pots – creates a sense of unity. Different shapes and styles can be drawn together by a theme of metal, terracotta or wire.

candles in pots

how to get the work done

Decorating a house involves commissioning a range of craftsmen, from plumbers, painters and builders to architects, furniture makers and restorers. Finding the right person to do the work is rarely easy, but it is always worth taking the extra time to contact at least three different companies to compare quotations, and to discuss their ideas. It's also extremely difficult to guarantee the quality of the work, although the steps below should help minimise the chance of problems.

The most important point to remember is that it is your house, and you will have to live with their work. Your perspective is not the same as the workmen, craftsmen and professionals you commission, and this can give you insights that they don't have. You owe it to yourself – and them – to stay in touch with ongoing work, to be clear about telling them what is most important to you, to take extra time to check every stage, not to assume anything – especially not that they can read your mind – and to make sure that they listen to your ideas. This doesn't mean turning yourself into the client from hell – a clear brief and a proper time frame, along with a fair structure of payment will be welcomed by any true professional.

■ Look for professionals, craftsmen or workmen who specialise in the kind of work you want carried out. For example, architects who work on listed buildings, or interior decorators experienced in country style or urban chic. The associations (see opposite) often keep lists of specific experts, and may also have 'briefing guidelines' they can send you. Word of mouth, local directories and newspapers are also good sources.

■ Look at past work or discuss former projects to ensure that you like their style. If you want an ultra-modern look, there's no point in commissioning a traditional designer, for example.

■ Explain what you have in mind and what your budget is. Give a clear idea of your daily life, how you live, and what you wish the work to achieve.

■ Write your brief down. Make sure that what you are asking can be understood – 'stunningly beautiful but practical' does not mean much, while 'pared-down country style with all domestic equipment concealed, yet easy to reach' gives a clear direction.

■ It is critical to check all plans and measurements in a way that makes sense to you. If the plans say 15 ft (3 m), for example, measure that out on the floor and see if it is the size you had envisaged. Check the size, style and position of anything major – eg doors, windows or radiators – ensuring the plans allows you flexibility when you come to furnishing. Mistakes are often made at this stage, and are expensive to correct once the work is done!

■ Be realistic about the time frame. Commissioning work is not the same as buying something from a shop – it will be weeks or months, not days. However, do make calls regularly to check progress and start or delivery dates. It helps prevent your job being sidelined for something more 'urgent'.

■ When restoring antiques or architectural salvage, don't risk amateur repairs. These can permanently damage the value. Find out all you can, and look for experts. Specialist departments of auction houses sometimes offer advice on whether repairs are possible without affecting the value, and may know suitable specialists you could contact.

■ Try out all colours, paints and wallpapers first in the largest possible patches or swatches on the wall to see what they look like in your room. Give yourself time to decide. If you're not clear about what something looks like (eg low voltage halogen lighting, specialist wood veneers), see if you can find an example in a friend's house or showroom roomset.

■ Ask for a scale of fees and a formal quotation of what the work will cost, and, if the initial plans and drawings are detailed, be prepared to pay for these separately. If you go ahead, the cost will often be deducted from the final bill. Work should be paid for in instalments – a deposit, money for materials, more as stages are completed, etc. Never pay the full amount upfront. Keep a small percentage back for 'snagging' – in other words, don't pay the last amount until you have done a final thorough check of the work. Then pay in full promptly. Most people work for themselves or for small companies, and cash flow is critical to their survival.

Useful addresses:

LAPADA (London & Provincial Antique Dealers Association)
535 King's Road
London SW10 0SZ
tel: 0171 823 3511
fax: 0171 823 3522
Association of 700 antique dealers who abide by their industry code of practice. For your nearest dealer contact them. Expertise in shipping abroad.

British Antique Dealers Association
20 Rutland Gate
London SW7 1BD
tel: 0171 589 4128
fax: 0171 581 9083
Advice on buying antiques, details of 400 members, expertise in shipping abroad.

The Architectural Salvage Index
c/o Hutton & Rostron
Netley House
Gomshall, Guildford
Surrey GU5 9QA
tel: 01483 203 221
Architectural register of items wanted to buy and sell.

The Interior Designers & Decorators Association
1-4 Chelsea Harbour
Design Centre
11 Lots Road
London SW10 0XE
tel: 0171 349 0800
Nationwide listings of interior designers and decorators.

Association of Master Upholsterers & Soft Furnishers
Frances Vaughan House
102a Commercial Street
Newport, Gwent NP9 1LU
tel: 01633 215 454
Lists of registered members.

British Antique Furniture Restorers Association
The Old Rectory
Warmwell, Dorchester
Dorset DT2 8HQ
tel: 01305 854 822
Furniture, marble, carving and gilding restorers.

English Heritage
23 Savile Row
London W1X 1AB
tel: 0171 973 3000
Advice on listed buildings and names of experts.

The Georgian Group
6 Fitzroy Square
London W1P 6DX
tel: 0171 387 1720
Leaflets and lectures on restoring Georgian properties.

The Crafts Council
44a Pentonville Road
London N1 9BY
tel: 0171 278 7700
Information on contemporary crafts in the U.K.

The Lighting Industry Federation
207 Balham High Road
London SW17 7BQ
tel: 0181 675 5432
Members are lighting manufacturers nationwide.

Royal Institute of British Architects
66 Portland Place
London W1N 4AD
tel: 0171 580 5533
Lists of architects and their specialities nationwide. For Scotland call the Royal Incorporation of Architects in Scotland tel: 0131 229 7545.

The Victorian Society
1 Priory Gardens
London W4 1TT
tel: 0181 994 1019
fax: 0181 995 4895
Leaflets on Victorian features, and all aspects of preserving original Victorian architecture. Walks, tours, lectures and other events.

directory

The furniture, lighting, storage, bedding and china featured on the 'Creating the look' pages came from the companies in this directory, and the architects and designers who worked on the various homes are also listed here. As stock changes regularly, we have not specified exactly where each item came from, but if you want to buy similar pieces, this directory lists the company speciality under the address. Those that do not have formal mail order catalogues will usually ship items nationwide when specified, and you can check in the Mail Order section for those offering full mail order services.

ANTIQUES

**The Decorative Antiques &
Textiles Fair** (twice yearly)
tel: 0171 624 5173

The Fine Art & Antiques Fair
(three times yearly)
tel: 0171 370 8211/8234

**The LAPADA Antiques &
Fine Art Fair**
tel: 0121 780 4141
fax: 0121 767 3540.

Julia Dickens
Grayshott Pine
Crossways Road
Grayshott, nr Hindhead
Surrey
Antiques and old pine.

ARCHITECTS AND DESIGNERS

Jason Cooper Architects
14 Alexander Street
London W2 5NT
tel/fax: 0171 727 3104
Architect.

Alastair Hendy
tel: 0171 739 5995
Food writer, stylist and designer
specialising in kitchens.

Christian Kyriacou
tel: 0181 541 1700
Feng shui architect.

James Lynch Design
City Lofts
112-116 Old Street
London EC1V 9BD
tel: 0171 336 6488
Design and development.

Melissa Merryweather
MS Merryweather
5 Panther House
38 Mount Pleasant
London WC1X OAN
tel: 0171 837 7030
Architect.

Gunnar Orefelt
Orefelt Associates Ltd
Portobello Studios
5 Haydens Place
London W11 1LY
tel: 0171 243 3181
fax: 0171 792 1126
e-mail: orefelt@msn.com
Architect.

Peter Romaniuk
The Flower House
Cynthia Street
London N1 9JF
tel: 0171 837 5490
Architect.

Christopher Spink
4 Becondale Road
London SE19 1QJ
tel: 0181 670 0081
Architect.

Barbara Weiss
4 Offord Street
London N1 1DH
tel: 0171 607 1867
fax: 0171 700 2952
Architect.

Stephen Woodhams
1 Aldwych
London WC2 4BZ
tel: 0171 300 0777
Garden and floral designer.

BATHROOM SPECIALISTS

Alternative Plans
9 Hester Road
London SW11 4AN
tel: 0171 228 6460
Contemporary bathrooms
and kitchens.

Aston Matthews
141-147 Essex Road
London N1 2SN
tel: 0171 226 3657
fax: 0171 354 5951
Large selection of cast iron and
other baths, plus showers, wide
range of sizes in basin, plus all
other bathroom equipment.

CP Hart
Newnham Terrace
Hercules Road
London SE1 7DR
tel: 0171 902 100
Extensive bathroom showroom
with wide range of traditional and
modern baths, showers, basins,
taps etc displayed in roomsets.

BEDS AND BEDDING

Bed Bazaar
The Old Station
Station Road
Framlingham
Suffolk IP13 9EE
tel: 01728 723 756
fax: 01728 724 626
Antique brass and iron beds, with
a sister company making
mattresses in any shape or size.

Designers Guild
(see Home Stores)
Contemporary bedlinen.

House of Steel (see Furniture)
Steel Furniture..

Inventory (see Home Stores)
Well priced, stylish bedlinen.

The Iron Bed Company
Southfield Park
Delling Lane
Bosham
Chichester, West Sussex
PO18 8NN
tel: 01243 574 049
fax: 01243 573 768
New iron beds based on
traditional and modern designs.
Mail order available.

Vi-Spring
Ernesettle
Plymouth
PL5 2TT
tel: 01752 366 311
fax: 01752 355 109
Beds, divan beds and mattresses
known for their comfort. This is a
trade supplier but they will
provide a list of local stockists.

CHILDREN
The Hill Toy Company
71 Abingdon Road
London W8 6AW
tel: 0171 937 8797
fax: 0171 937 0209
Tents, dressing up clothes,
dolls' houses and other toys.

The Lazy Lizard
(see Mail Order companies)
Child-sized chairs, sofas and
soft furnishings with toyboxes
incorporated.

Shelfstore
6/8 Frognal Parade
158 Finchley Road
London NW3 5HH
tel: 0171 794 0313
Storage and bunk bed/desk
systems.

CONSERVATORY AND GARDEN
ROOM SPECIALISTS
Appeal Blinds
6 Vale Lane
Bedminster
Bristol BS3 5SD
tel: 0117 963 7734
fax: 0117 966 6216
Specialist blinds for conservatories.

George Carter
Silverstone Farm
North Elmham
Norfolk NR20 5EX
tel: 01362 668 130
Garden structures in wood, such as
'sentry box' garden shed.

The Cast Iron Shop
394 Caledonian Road
London N1 1DW
tel: 0171 609 0934
fax: 0171 607 7565
Ornate iron benches and chairs.

**Lloyd Christie Garden
Architecture**
1 New Kings Road
London SW6 4SB
tel: 0171 731 3484
Bespoke conservatories and
garden structures.

Courtyard Designs
Suckley
Worcester WR6 5EH
tel: 01886 884 640
fax: 01886 884 444
'Office in the garden' range of
timber offices that can often be
erected without planning
permission, with power, lighting,
security and communications. Also
sheds, summerhouses and garages.

The English Garden Collection
tel: 0870 606 0304
Garden equipment, outdoor
living, furniture, lanterns and pots.

Marston & Langinger
192 Ebury Street
London SW1W 8UP
tel: 0171 824 8818
Conservatory manufacturer and
supplier of conservatory furniture,
lighting and pots, mail order also.

Stephen Woodhams
1 Aldwych
London WC2 4BZ
tel 0171 300 0777
Garden and floral design, pot
and conservatory accessories,
garden design.

FIXTURES AND FITTINGS
Artisan
4a Union Court, 20 Union Road,
London SW4 6JP
tel: 0171 498 6974
Curtain poles and finials in a
wide range of styles.

The Cast Iron Shop
(see Conservatories)
Balusters, gates, staircases, railings.

Handles and Fittings Ltd
HAF House, Mead Lane
Hertford, Herts SG13 7AP
tel: 01992 505 655
Steel and brass contemporary
handles and hardware.

CP Hart (See Bathroom Specialists)
Taps, sanitaryware.

Nu Line
317 Westbourne Park Road
London W11
tel: 0171 727 7748
Fixtures and fittings for kitchens,
including handles, spring catches.

Tidmarsh
1 Lacock Street, London N1 1SW
tel: 0171 226 2261
Wooden blinds.

FURNITURE
Aero
96 Westbourne Grove
London W2 5RT
tel: 0171 221 1950
fax: 0171 221 2555
Contemporary furniture
and accessories, mail order
also available.

Bombay Duck
231 The Vale, London W3 7QS
tel: 0181 749 8001
e-mail info@bombayduck.co.uk
Conservatory-style wrought
iron furniture.

Coast Collection
tel: 0171 378 8591
Contemporary furniture
and accessories;
commissions welcome

Crispin & Gemma
Furniture Design
85 Essex Road, London N1 2SF
tel: 0171 226 8074
Curved wooden furniture
including filing cabinets.

Grand Illusions
2-4 Crown Road
St Margarets, Twickenham
Middlesex TW1 3EE
tel: 0181 744 1046
Painted and wooden furniture,
lighting and paints.

House of Steel
400 Caledonian Road
London N1 1DN
tel/fax: 0171 607 5889
Steel furniture.

Corin Mellor
c/o David Mellor
4 Sloane Square
London SW1W 8EE
tel: 0171 730 4259
Sculptural forms in
moulded birch.

Charles Page
61 Fairfax Road, Swiss Cottage
London NW6 4EE
tel: 0171 328 9851
Quality furniture and
interior design.

Purves & Purves
80-81 & 83 Tottenham
Court Road
London W1P 9HD
tel: 0171 580 8223
fax: 0171 580 8244
Contemporary furniture.

SCP
135-139 Curtain Road
London EC2A 3BX
tel: 0171 739 1869
fax: 0171 729 4224
Contemporary furniture,
including Jasper Morrison,
Matthew Hilton, and
Konstantin Grcic.

Shaker
25 Harcourt Street
London W1H 1DT
tel: 0171 724 7672
fax: 0171 724 6640
Shaker furniture and accessories.

Trannon Furniture
Childhampton Farm
Wilton
Salisbury SP2 0AB
tel: 01722 744 577
Contemporary wooden
furniture, including stacking
tables and chairs.

Viaduct
1-10 Summer's Street
London EC1R 5BD
tel: 0171 278 8456
fax: 0171 278 2884
Modern classics: Driade, Philippe
Starck and others.

Wireworks
131a Broadley Street
London NW8 8BA
tel: 0171 724 8856
Wire and metal furniture
and accessories.

FLOORING

Amtico
Kingfield Road
Coventry CV6 5PL
tel: 01203 861 400 for
local stockists.
Trade suppliers of Amtico.

Crucial Trading
The Market Hall, Craven Arms
Shropshire SY7 9NF
tel: 01588 673 666
Natural flooring, sisal,
coir and seagrass.

Edelman Leather
C&G Partnership
43 Kilmaine Road
London SW16 7JU
tel/fax: 0171 610 0855
Leather flooring.

Fired Earth
Twyford Mill
Oxford Road, Adderbury
Oxon OX17 3HP
tel: 01295 812 088
fax: 01295 810 832
Tiled flooring.

Forbo-Nairn
PO Box 1
Kirkaldy, Fife KY1 2SB
tel: 01592 643 111
Trade suppliers of linoleum and
marmoleum, call for local stockists.

Roger Oates Design
The Long Barn
Eastnor, Ledbury
Herefordshire HR8 1EL
tel: 01531 632 718
Wool carpets.

Pergo Flooring
Perstorp Flooring UK
18-19 Cromwell Park
Chipping Norton
Oxfordshire OX7 5SR
tel: 0800 374 771
Hard-wearing laminated flooring
in a selection of wood designs.

Sinclair Till
791-793 Wandsworth Road
London SW8 3JQ
tel: 0171 720 0031
fax: 0171 498 3814
Specialists in linoleum,
wood flooring, mattings,
carpets and rugs.

HOME STORES

Aero
96 Westbourne Grove
London W2 5RT
tel: 0171 221 1950
Also see mail order. Contemporary
furniture and accessories.

The Conran Shop
Michelin House
81 Fulham Road
London SW3 6RD
tel:0171 589 7401
fax: 0171 823 7015
Contemporary furniture
and design.

Designers Guild
267-271 King's Road
London SW3 5EN
tel: 0171 243 7300
fax: 0171 243 7710
Home store with a reputation for
contemporary colour. Fabrics,
wallpapers, furniture, china and
accessories, bedlinen.

Habitat
196 Tottenham Court Road
London W1P 9LD
For local branches:
tel: 0645 334 433
Contemporary furniture,
accessories and bedlinen.

Heals
196 Tottenham Court Road
London W1P 9LD
tel: 0171 636 1666
Contemporary furniture,
bedlinen, lighting and china.

The Home Place
The Hyde, Edgware
London NW9 7TH
tel: 0181 200 5588
Bathroom and kitchen accessories,
lighting and bedding.

House of Fraser
department stores
1 Howick Place
London SW1P 1BH
tel: 0171 963 2000
Furniture, kitchen accessories,
lighting and bedding.

IKEA
Brent Park
2 Drury Way
North Circular Road
London NW10 OTH
For nationwide stores:
tel: 0181 208 5600
Swedish furniture group
known for its well priced
self-assembly furniture.

Inventory
26-40 Kensington High Street
London W84 4PF
tel: 0171 937 2626
Home accessories including
bedding, lighting and china.

Laura Ashley
For stores nationwide:
tel: 0990 622 116
Fashion and furnishings. Fabric
company with furniture, china
and bathroom accessories.

MUJI
26 Great Marlborough Street
London W1V 1HL
For information and
other branches:
tel: 0171 494 1197
Minimalist 'no name' Japanese
storage, kitchenware, fashion and
miscellaneous items including
office furniture.

The Pier
153 Milton Park
Abingdon
Oxon OX14 4SD
tel: 0171 637 7001
Wicker furniture, tables and
contemporary accessories.

KITCHEN SPECIALISTS
Aga-Rayburn
P.O. Box 30
Ketley, Telford
Shropshire TF1 4DD
tel: 01952 642 000
fax: 01952 641 961
Kitchen range and cast-iron
stove specialists.

American Appliance Centre
52 Larkshall Road
Chingford
London E4 6PD
tel: 0181 529 9665
Extra large American
refrigerators. Trade supplier only.

Appliance World
145 Faringdon Road
Swindon
Wilts, SN1 5DL
tel: 01793 422 300
Delivery nationwide of American
fridges and cookers.

Britannia steel ranges:
stocked by **John Lewis**
(tel: 0171 629 7711 for branches)
and **Harrods** (tel: 0171 730 1234)

Mark Brook
tel: 0171 221 8106
Kitchen designer.

Buyers & Sellers
120-122 Ladbroke Grove
London W10 5NE
tel: 0171 229 1947
Discount domestic
electrical appliances.

IKEA (see Home Stores)

John Lewis of Hungerford
Park Street
Hungerford
Berkshire RG17 OEA
tel: 01488 682 066
Handmade fitted and freestanding
wooden kitchens.

David Mellor
4 Sloane Square
London SW1W 8EE
tel: 0171 730 4259
Designer kitchen shop with
contemporary cutlery and
fine pottery.

Smallbone Kitchens
105 Fulham Road
London SW3 6RL
tel: 0171 589 5998
Handmade fitted and free-standing
kitchen furniture in traditional and
contemporary styles.

Smeg
Corinthian Court
80 Milton Park
Abingdon, Oxon OX14 4RY
tel: 01235 861 090
Stainless steel and colour freezers.

WORK SURFACES
Laminates: **Formica Ltd**
tel: 0191 259 3000

Recycled plastic: **Made of Waste**
tel: 0171 278 6971

Stainless steel: **Anchor Food
Service Equipment**
tel: 01322 335 544

Tiles: **World End Tiles**
tel: 0171 720 8358

Wood: **The Hardwood Flooring
Company**
tel: 0171 328 8481

LIGHTING AND ELECTRICS
Best & Lloyd
William Street West
Smethwick, Warley
West Midlands B66 2NX
tel: 0121 558 1191
fax: 0121 565 3547
Suppliers of classic Bestlite,
lighting, swing arm wall
brackets, picture lights and
bathroom lighting.

John Cullen Lighting
585 King's Road
London SW6 2EH
tel: 0171 371 5400
Lighting design and fittings.

London Lighting Company
135 Fulham Road
London SW3 2RT
tel: 0171 589 3612
fax: 0171 581 9652
Lighting showroom with a good
selection of contemporary lighting.

Mr Light
279 King's Road
London SW3 5EW
tel: 0171 352 8398
fax: 0171 351 3484
Good selection of
contemporary lighting.

MAIL ORDER COMPANIES:
Aero
tel: 0181 871 4030
Contemporary furniture.

Bombay Duck (see Furniture)
tel: 0181 749 8001
e-mail info@bombayduck.co.uk
Decorative home accessories and
wrought-iron furniture.

The English Garden Collection
tel: 0870 606 0304
Pots, gardening accessories and
outdoor living.

Grand Illusions (see Furniture)
tel 0181 744 1046
Painted and wooden furniture.

The Hill Toy Company
tel: 01765 689 955
Toys, tents and dressing up.

The Holding Company
tel: 0171 610 9160
Storage for every room.

The Iron Bed Company
tel: 01243 574 049
Wide range of iron bed designs.

Lazy Lizard
tel: 0171 622 4561
e-mail: Lazychairs@aol.com
Child-size sofas and chairs.

Marston & Langinger
tel: 0171 824 8818
Conservatories and furniture.

Andrew Martin Direct
tel: 0800 328 1346
Bedlinen and bath accessories.

Ocean
tel: 0800 132 985
Contemporary accessories
and storage.

Paperchase
tel: 0171 580 8496
Storage and stationery.

MIRRORS, PICTURES AND
MISCELLANEOUS DECORATIVE
ACCESSORIES
Avant Garden
77 Ledbury Road
London W11 2AG
tel: 0171 229 4408
Pots and wirework
including topiary.

**Michael Hoppen
Photographers Gallery**
3 Jubilee Place
London SW3 3TD
tel: 0171 352 3649
Photographic gallery
specialising in early and modern
photographic prints.

Joseph Maison
26 Sloane Street
London SW1X 7LQ
tel: 0171 245 9493
Maryse Boxer china and glass.

Ocean (see Mail Order)

OFFICE EQUIPMENT
Bite Communications
5 Albion Court, Galena Road
London W6 0QT
tel: 0181 741 1123
fax: 0181 563 1324
Computer equipment.

Habitat (see Home Stores)
Home office desks, chairs, tables
and storage.

The Holding Company
(see Storage)
Office storage, desks and
document boxes.

IKEA (see Home Stores)
Home office desks, chairs, storage.

MUJI (see Home stores)
Home office desks, chairs, tables
and storage.

Paperchase
213 Tottenham Court Road
London W1P 9AF
tel: 0171 580 8496
fax: 0171 637 1225
Stationery suppliers with
nationwide branches and
mail order.

PAINTS AND WALLPAPER
Brats
281 King's Road
London SW3 5EW
tel: 0171 351 7675
fax: 0171 349 8644
'Mediterranean' paints.

Dulux
Retail Advice Centre
tel: 01753 550 555
Manufacturer of a wide range of
paints, including Heritage colours
and paint mixing services.

Farrow & Ball
33 Uddens Trading Estate
Wimborne, Dorset BH21 7NL
tel: 01202 876 141
fax:01202 873 793
National Trust historic paints.

Papers and Paints
4 Park Walk
London SW10 OAD
tel: 0171 352 8626
fax: 0171 352 1017
Paints and paint matching service.

Sanderson
tel: 0171 584 3344 for stockists
Over 1200 shades of paint.

SOFT FURNISHINGS
Celia Birtwell
71 Westbourne Park Road
London W2 5QH
tel: 0171 221 0877
Sheers, unusual fabrics, gold
printing and soft colours.

Joseph Maison
26 Sloane Street
London SW1X 7LQ
tel: 0171 245 9493
Maryse Boxer china and gifts,
cutlery, Carolyn Quatermaine
fabrics and gilt furniture.

Malabar
Unit 31-33
South Bank Business Centre
Ponton Road
London SW8 5BL
tel: 0171 501 4200
fax: 0171 501 4210
Cottons, silks and sheers.

Ian Mankin
109 Regents Park Road
London NW1 8UR
tel: 0171 722 0997
fax: 0171 722 2159
Checked and striped fabrics.

Andrew Martin
200 Walton Street
London SW3 2JL
tel: 0171 584 4290
Prints, weaves and wallpaper, also
bedlinens, and reproduction and
oriental furniture.

Geraldine Paine
23 Tudor Gardens
Twickenham
Middlesex TW1 4LE
tel: 0181 892 0833
Soft furnishings specialist:
makes up curtains, loose covers
and blinds.

Peter Harvey London Ltd
2 Bridge Studios
Wandsworth Bridge Road
Fulham SW6 2TZ
tel: 0171 736 3311
Contemporary furniture,
accessories and lighting.

Tessallato Textiles
89 Shore Road
Strangford
Co Down BT30 7NW
tel:(0)1396 881 683
Hand-dyed bed linen.

STORAGE
The Holding Company
243 Kings Road
London SW3 5EL
tel: 0171 352 1600
Office storage.

Habitat
(see Home Stores)

IKEA
(See Home Stores)

Shelfstore
(see Mail Order)
Desk, shelf and bunk bed kits that
can be adapted to your layout.

index

Page numbers in bold refer to refer to illustrations.

acknowledgements

The houses in this book belong to people – many of them friends –
who have had the vision to create inspirational homes which are
also wonderful to live in. We'd like to thank them for allowing us to
photograph them.

We would also like to thank Cindy Richards, Kate Haxell and
Christine Wood from Collins & Brown; our agent, Sarah Molloy
of AM Heath; and our families.